DEE[

Through a Tracker's Eyes

Paul C. Carter

Printed by CreateSpace, an Amazon company.

Cover photograph by Charles C. Carter

DEDICATION

To Larry Benoit—
expert tracker and deer hunter; gone but not forgotten.
For me, an inspirational figure who was instrumental in
changing my style of hunting for the better.

TABLE OF CONTENTS

PREFACE

Ever since I was a young boy I enjoyed hearing hunting stories. Naturally, for a New Englander like me, the bulk of these tales involved the whitetail deer as the principal animal of interest. My father, his contemporaries, and even a few individuals counted among the generation immediately preceding theirs were the most frequent story tellers. As I raptly absorbed every detail, I could only imagine the day when I would be old enough to participate in the fall hunts. More than anything, I wanted to become a member of this fraternity and hunt deer. In the late 1960s I finally realized my goal.

Now, some forty-five years later, I am fortunate to possess a veritable lifetime of hunting stories of my own making. For those readers who aren't familiar with me, my hunting method of choice is tracking deer in snow. Without being snobbish, I happen to believe that tracking, because of its very active nature, lends itself perfectly to interesting narrative. It's taken some time, but I was finally persuaded to put some of the deer hunting sagas I've enjoyed to print. My very first book, *Tracking Whitetails: Answers to Your Questions*, can be described as a "how-to" work. My intention here is quite different.

The stories contained herein are all derived from my personal hunting experiences and selected primarily for their entertainment value. Included in the mix are hunts of all types: successful outcomes, failures, those involving big bucks and many where smaller bucks and even does were central to the plot. In all cases, I've tried to be as forthright as memory allows and not embellish the particulars. Even so, in a few rare instances, I've been a party to activities that may strain credulity. Rest assured; any such portrayals are accurate, and they make for interesting reading.

In some places, where I could do so without interrupting the flow of the story, I deliberately included a tip or insight, or highlighted a specific course of action in order to help other aspiring trackers deal with similar situations. Finally, in some instances I've intentionally omitted the names of certain individuals. This was done for one of the following reasons: to shield the person from embarrassment or to protect the location of my hunting area.

One last thing: What follows is not a chronological history of my deer hunting career. I chose that approach for my book, *Sheep Hunts: One Man's Journeys to the High Country*, because I desired to document my personal odyssey and evolution as a sheep hunter. As I previously stated, my primary goal this time is one of entertainment. With that objective in mind, many tales, whether resulting in success or not, have been purposefully omitted. The remaining ones, the accounts which made the cut, are presented in no particular order.

BEGINNINGS

I was in high school when I, at long last, met the legal requirements to hunt deer as mandated by the state of Massachusetts. The Hunter Safety course was the center-piece of my formal instruction. At the time, I'm sure I didn't fully appreciate the course's important role in preventing accidental shootings, nor did I adequately recognize the efforts of the volunteers who served as instructors. Before I could hunt, though, I also had to satisfy my father that I could be trusted to handle a shotgun with respect, good judgment and, at all times, the safety of others in mind.

When I first entered the deer woods in 1968, things were quite different than they are today. First, deer popula-tions in my home state were at a modern-day low ebb. Decades of an either-sex policy, combined with a string of unusually severe winters, had taken its toll on the local deer herds. In many places it was rare to find deer tracks, and rarer still were deer sightings. The state had recently adopt-ed a bucks-only management policy, which was intended to restore the animal's depleted population. A few highly val-ued so-called "doe" permits were issued each year, allowing lucky recipients a better opportunity to take home venison.

It was against this backdrop that I began my deer hunting career. For many years, I had been reading every story pertaining to whitetails in the hunting magazines of the era, like *Outdoor Life* and *Field & Stream*. I wanted to kill a deer in the worst way. And according to those articles, the best way to accomplish my objective was to take a stationary position in the woods and let the deer come to me. Generally, small-scale deer drives were the tactic of choice for our hunting group. At first, older and more experienced members of the hunting party decided where I should stand. I never saw any deer, but I regularly became cold to the point of shivering by the time each push concluded.

Eventually, in the wake of seemingly endless disappointment, I came to the conclusion that I couldn't do any worse if I walked through the woods instead of posting up. If nothing else, I'd have a better chance of staying reasonably warm. And as I quickly learned, my sudden turn to mobility had other benefits: I began to understand the blocks of woods in which I hunted in a way that had been impossible before; I developed a sense of confidence in my ability to navigate in the forest; and I witnessed more wildlife and the sign they left behind. I even saw a deer on occasion. Admittedly, in almost every instance, I was only able to view the deer's signature raised tail flashing through the brush to my front, as it catapulted out of sight.

A full decade had passed since I first started hunting and I still hadn't killed a deer. However, during that same period of time, my efforts had been integral to other members of our party tagging deer. As my role of head "dog" became more entrenched, deer I jumped from their beds during my excursions met their demise at the hand of others in our group with increasing regularity. I took great pride in my contributions and success was always exhilarating, even if I hadn't been the one to pull the trigger. On one such drive in 1977, Billy Drew killed a mature, eight-point buck I had rousted from his bed. That deer was the first racked buck I had ever seen, not counting pictures in magazines and mounts on walls.

I finally killed my very first deer on Thanksgiving morning in 1979. I shot the buck fawn with an old Browning recurve bow, as I stood behind a large hemlock tree. Although I haven't bow hunted in years, I was doing so during that period in order to spend more time in the woods. My long drought may have been broken, but come shotgun season I still wanted nothing to do with hunting from a stand, even though the tactic had been instrumental in taking my first whitetail.

My evolution to becoming the hunter I am today would continue. By 1980, I was a self-described walker. Although I was happy to follow deer when snow was present, I didn't consider myself to truly be a tracker. After all, to that point I had only taken a single deer, and the thought of purposefully killing an animal whose track I was dogging seemed too difficult, something well beyond my skill set. I was, however, increasingly interested in the prospect.

As the years passed, my ability to discern the small details needed to successfully track deer vastly improved. I was pretty good at aging tracks, distinguishing between those made by bucks and does, and correlating track size to body weight. And the number of acres of land that I was intimately familiar with had expanded greatly. My remaining deficiencies were related to the "end" game. That is, getting reasonably close to stationary deer and seeing them before they ran off.

I had long ago purchased Larry Benoit's book, *How to Bag the Biggest Buck of Your Life*, which I made sure to read at the start of each hunting season, just to psych myself up. Besides the emotional lift the book provided each fall, it opened my eyes to what was possible in the woods. If others could single out a particular buck and hunt it down, then why couldn't I? Nearly twenty years after my initial foray as a neophyte deer hunter, I accomplished something I wouldn't even have dreamed possible way back then. What follows is the story of that seminal event in my life as a white-tail hunter.

++++++++

The 1986 deer season was rapidly slipping away. Our annual trip to New Hampshire in November had been productive, as I had blundered into a hefty spike-horn buck that hung around too long after hearing me approach from the backside of his chosen bedding spot. The deer stood up and faced me, substantially shielded by a large tree. The buck decided to stay put rather than fleeing, even after my first shot missed its mark. My second shot dropped him in his tracks. The Massachusetts shotgun season had passed without much in the way of action, which left only the three-day primitive firearms season for me to connect on a deer. The first two-thirds of that season had been unremarkable, as well, as the ground continued to be bare of snow.

The nightly weather forecast hadn't predicted any frozen precipitation, but when I woke for the final day's hunt, the ground was covered with three inches of freshly fallen wet snow. That was a very welcome surprise, indeed, and it helped to counter-balance my growing concern that I was on the verge of becoming ill with some sort of upper respiratory condition. The snow had stopped falling just before dawn, ensuring that any tracks I might find would be exceedingly fresh.

At the time, you could kill a deer of either sex during the muzzleloader season. However, the rules regarding what constituted a legal weapon were a little strange. My state mandated that hunters could only employ percussion or flintlock arms possessing a smooth bore. What the authorities had against rifling, I did not know. The regulation was so unique that Thompson/Center Arms, located in neighboring New Hampshire, produced a muzzleloader specifically for Massachusetts hunters—a fifty-six caliber smoothbore. Furthermore, patched round balls were the only approved projectiles. Especially when compared to modern muzzleloaders, the performance obtainable from such a combination left a lot to be desired, in regards to both accuracy and range. At fifty yards the guns were okay; from a distance of 100 yards, bullet energy was marginal and it was hard to know exactly where your ball might hit.

I had been hunting an area not too far from my home. Deer seemed to be reasonably plentiful there and I figured the new snow could only improve my chances for success. So rather than heading for new ground, I decided to give the place one last try. I intended to begin my hunt where an old logging header intersected an unimproved dirt road. At this location, I could park my truck and then ascend the old skid trail in search of tracks.

The day didn't get off to a very good start, though. As I was approaching my destination, with my truck in four-wheel drive, something unexpected happened. I was slowly motoring up a small hill when I suddenly began to slide backwards! One minute I was advancing; the next minute I was in an un-controlled retreat. Apparently, the snow had obscured a sheet of ice. After nearly thirty yards of a panic-inducing slide, the truck's rear wheels managed to grip the road's ice-less shoulder, which caused the out-of-control vehicle to spin counter-clockwise about ninety degrees. From there, I was able to point the truck downhill, retrace my tire tracks and park at a location that, while requiring slightly more walking, posed far less of a threat to my health.

I took a deep breath, performed a quick check of my underwear, and exited the truck. The near accident had sowed some doubts for a few anxious seconds, but it looked like I was going to be able to hunt after all. I proceeded to place a percussion cap on the nipple of my gun before starting back towards the hill. I still needed to safely navigate that hazardous little incline before I could access the logging road, though. I carefully stayed well off the road proper, making sure to test each step before transferring my weight.

I began my hike up the well-defined skid trail, keeping an eye out for deer tracks as I made my way higher. A half mile up the mountain, where the terrain leveled somewhat, the road forked. I chose the branch that headed west towards a small brook. It was near the junction of the brook and the secondary skid road that I discovered three very fresh deer tracks, headed higher. After examining the prints carefully, I concluded that the makers were does and a single fawn. That there were apparently no antlered bucks in the small group was of little concern.

The animals were clearly undisturbed and, as far as I could tell, no other hunters were in the immediate area. Based on the razor-sharp definition exhibited by the spoor, I assumed the deer weren't too far ahead of me. I figured they were probably bedded on one of the numerous knolls that graced the upper reaches of the mountain. Acting accordingly, I slowed my pace to a veritable crawl. I'd take a single step as quietly as possible, stop, and then search every piece of woods that was within view before repeating the process. This tedious but essential effort continued for a couple of hundred yards, as the deer paralleled the waterway on its western bank.

When the group turned and started walking along the hill's contour, I altered my technique somewhat. To this point, I had been walking over the same ground the deer had previously utilized, more or less. I now elected to climb about thirty yards above the tracks, tracing a higher contour than my quarry had taken.

As a general rule, deer bed on high spots in hilly country. From there, they can see a predator if it approaches along their back-track. At the same time, the animals can use their sense of smell and the prevailing wind to warn them about danger coming from a different direction.

Paralleling the tracks from a higher vantage point presumably put me thirty yards closer to the deer, and it also eliminated some of the hill's convexity, allowing me a better chance to see them. These subtle changes just might make the difference between getting a good shooting opportunity and never firing the gun when the moment of truth arrived.

Although I had elected to modify my tactics slightly, I continued to maintain my snail-like pace as I advanced. After another 100 yards of painstaking progress, I thought I heard something above me, over a small rise. I froze in place, my gun at the ready. Seconds passed before I was able to conclusively identify the source of the noise as a walking animal. Before long, I could see deer legs through the brush, about seventy yards up the hill. It looked like I was about to get my long-awaited chance.

I knew that any misstep at this critical juncture would surely cost me the deer. I carefully cocked the side hammer on the muzzleloader, making sure that I did so without creating a sound. That task complete, I slowly raised the gun to my shoulder in anticipation of the deer's next move. It wasn't necessary to confirm the presence of antlers, so I concentrated on finding an unobstructed path for my bullet to reach the animal's vitals. The deer took another step or two, and I suddenly had the window I had been seeking. When the sights looked perfect, I finished my trigger pull.

The deer instantly whirled back in the direction from which it had come and disappeared from sight. As the low-pitched "boom" of the muzzleloader receded, the sound was replaced with that of running deer. At the same time, the air was momentarily filled with a thick sulfurous haze, a by-product of the black powder that had just been ignited. As I stood in place, preparing to re-arm the muzzleloader, I heard what I thought to be a deer crashing into dead branches.

With the primitive firearm ready for action once again, I eagerly climbed to where the deer had last stood.

The blood sign was distinctive and profuse. A fine red spray coating the snow on both sides of the deer's path of retreat indicated my ball had center-punched the animal's chest, just as I had expected. I knew the tracking effort would be a short one. In a matter of minutes, I found the mature doe piled up in some brush less than eighty yards away. A second shot wasn't needed. I had done it: I had actually killed a deer while tracking!

Curious about the exact circumstances surrounding my success, I performed a little reconnaissance before attending to the doe. As best as I could tell, the group had chosen this place to bed for the day. However, I only found one bed, which seemed to indicate that the other two deer hadn't yet settled down at the time of my arrival. It's not unusual for deer to mill around their bedding area for a few minutes before lying down. While not provable, I suspect the doe heard my approach, despite my best efforts to walk silently, and came to investigate. It's equally possible that she was merely grabbing a few last mouthfuls of food before settling down for the day.

I returned to the dead doe, removed her entrails and headed back to the nearest logging road. The drag would prove to be a "piece of cake," as it was all downhill. The euphoria of success was rapidly being replaced by an increasingly sore throat, a running nose and muscle aches, however. As I had feared, I was getting sicker by the minute. No matter, I already had my prize; I could suffer my infirmity and still maintain an ear-to-ear grin. When I reached my truck it wasn't yet 10am.

As I reflected on the hunt in the days that followed, the pride I felt regarding my accomplishment only grew stronger. I had, on my own, taken up a track and killed its maker. No one was there to assist me. In fact, no other hunters impacted the outcome in any way. The contest had been distilled to the essentials: a wary animal on its home turf and a human interloper with inferior senses, superior cognitive abilities and a black-powder gun. For me, the whole experience engendered a sense of purity that had eluded me to this point.

Admittedly, the conditions had been perfect, and this tracking effort was neither the longest nor the most difficult in recorded history. Yet, it's impossible to ignore just how important this hunt was in my progression as a deer hunter. For the moment, this tracking kill was a singular success—the sole chapter in a still unwritten book, if you will. But, the accomplishment had breached an important threshold, and it helped me envision what my ultimate capabilities could prove to be.

In the years that followed, additional deer would meet the same end as this doe, proof positive that this hunt hadn't been merely a fluke and that tracking was my true destiny. Whether small bucks, mature bucks or does, each represented a unique set of circumstances and each required something different of me. But, it all started with this muzzle-loader doe. After December of 1986, I possessed a new-found sense of confidence and I wholeheartedly embraced my role as a self-described tracker.

Commonwealth of Massachusetts
Department of Fisheries, Wildlife &
Environmental Law Enforcement
Hunter Education Program
CERTIFICATE

NAME ...Paul Carter...

ADDRESS ...400 Grange Hall Rd. Dalton,
MA
DATE OF BIRTH... █████████ **ZIP** ...01226..........

The above named has successfully completed the course
in the safe handling of firearms approved by this Division.
Director,

H   4841   Division of Law Enforcement

Approved by

...........Sgt. Joseph Lynch............. DUPLICATE

...........October 21, 1968...............
DATE
...........Regional High School, Dalton, MA
LOCATION

....

NOT VALID UNLESS SIGNED BY STUDENT

*My hunter education certificate. I could finally hunt on my own. I misplaced
the original, but obtained this duplicate decades later.*

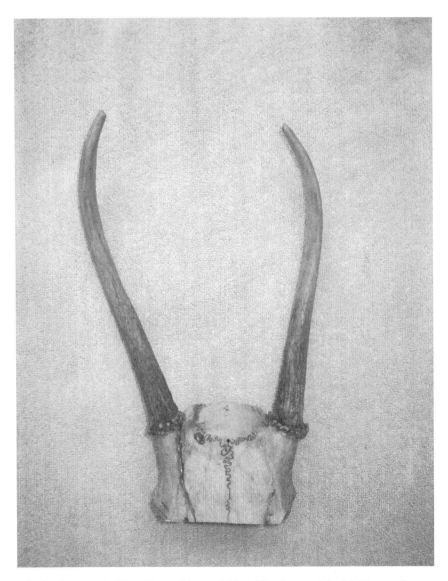

The buck I shot in New Hampshire in 1986. The deer weighed 145 pounds, but his antlers were poor for his size and age.

My very first whitetail deer, taken with a bow on Thanksgiving morning in 1979.

Photo by Charles Carter

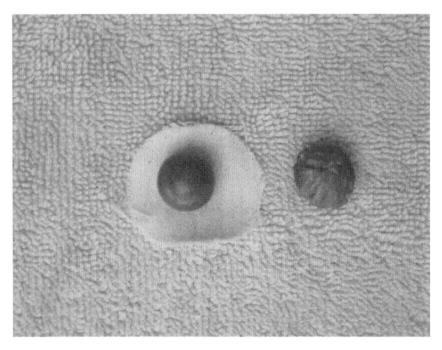

Ah, the good old days! Patched .56 caliber round balls in a non-rifled barrel.
The ball on the right was recovered from another deer I killed.

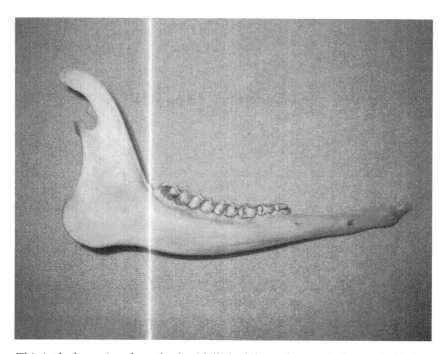

This is the lower jaw from the doe I killed while tracking. Tooth wear indicates she was 3 1/2 years old.

Lose One, Win One

Starting in the late 1960s, several members of our loosely knit local hunting group began to hunt deer in New Hampshire each fall. The seemingly ageless Billy Drew had long-standing connections there that dated to the 1920s. He finally convinced my father and Al Cady to come up and hunt. Although I was still in high school at the time of our inaugural foray, I was thrilled to be a party to the exploration of new hunting grounds.

Initially, we stayed at Hazen Morey's camp. After a few years, however, Hazen sold my father and Al a small piece of adjoining land, where they eventually placed a used trailer home. For more than forty years, one place or the other served as our base of operations for the November hunting season.

Each fall, several hunters native to Massachusetts made the pilgrimage to the steep terrain east of the Connecticut River valley. My father, Al, Billy and I were regular participants from my neck of the woods. We were usually joined by Bob Donnelly and his sons Bill and Butch, all of whom resided nearby. Over the years, there were numerous additions and subtractions to the group, but the aforementioned individuals constituted the core of our hunting party.

We took a few deer over the decades, but we never made too big a dent in the herd. The woods were big and we frequently had to do without snow, which tended to make the hunting difficult. Nevertheless, we never failed to have a good time. Card playing, tall tales and practical jokes were all part of the fun. Some great memories were created and shared over these years, not to mention the lasting friendships that developed.

It was on one of these hunts, before my tracking skills were more fully developed, that I had the opportunity to track a mature buck in the big woods which surrounded our camp. Initially, we jumped the buck from his bed during an early morning push. Bill Donnelly actually saw the deer, but he couldn't get off a shot. I got on the track later that morning and stayed on it for the rest of the day.

That buck took me on quite a tour, encompassing miles of forest. As I persistently followed, I really never felt that I was getting close to the deer. He didn't seem to want to lie down, nor did he seem anxious to stop so he could get a better look at his pursuer. The buck just maintained a decent pace as he traced a fairly large circle.

For my part, as the afternoon wore on and the miles began to accumulate, my feet became increasingly sore, as did the muscles of my neck and shoulders. I was relieved when I noticed that the deer was finally headed back in the general direction of the road where our camp was located.

In the course of this return swing, the buck chose to go around the backside of a large lake that dominated the landscape. Although I had never set foot in this particular area, I knew the aforementioned road was no more than a mile away. With daylight dwindling, I expected to either follow the deer to the road or leave the track if the buck elected to climb the steeper terrain to the north of the pond.

Once behind the lake, the buck walked through a dense stand of conifers. The young trees were a little more than head high and packed closely together. Even so, it was still possible to traverse the twenty-yard maze standing upright, but just barely. I plowed through the tangle as quickly as I could. As soon as I entered the decidedly more open ground on the far side, I heard the unmistakable sound of a deer starting to sprint. Almost simultaneously, I briefly eyed the hindquarters of the buck I had been tracking all these hours disappear up the hill. Although it had taken most of the day, I had been given a chance to kill this deer. Unfortunately, I had blown the opportunity!

I kicked myself for being so careless, but I wasn't overly disappointed. Even if I had been more cautious, I still might not have gotten a good shot at the deer. Besides, this particular location offered no easy routes to get a dead buck out of the woods.

To be honest, by the time of this encounter, I was weary and I had already resigned myself to the fact that I wasn't going to get a look at this particular deer. Furthermore, I had assumed—hoped even—that the buck would take me back to the road, where the lateness of the day would end the hunt. With the buck on the run again, only one real option remained. I left the deer, skirted the edge of the lake to the road, and made it back to camp just at dark.

I relate this story of failure because it holds some valuable lessons for would-be trackers. First, it's not uncommon that your best (and possibly only) chance to kill a buck you're following arrives at the end of the day when fatigue (mental and physical) is at a premium. To have any chance for success, you simply must maintain your highest state of vigilance for every minute that you're on the track. You just never know when an opportunity might present itself and you must always be ready, regardless of how sore your body is or how much your head aches from searching the brush for sign of the animal you're following. Once your concentration falters, you might as well bag the day and head home.

While this hunt helped reinforce the need for complete concentration on the task at hand, perhaps the most valuable lesson I took from the experience relates to features of terrain. Since this episode, I've been faced with other situations where a buck I was tracking passed through a thicket of dense, almost impenetrable, evergreens. Without exception, before emerging on the far side, I always stop inside the cover and scan the surrounding woods for the deer I'm following. While falling well short of being a sure thing, this prudent approach has been instrumental in netting me two top-end bucks over the years. What follows is the tale of one of those hunts.

++++++++

It was a cold and windy day in December 1994. Although the weather wasn't extreme, the conditions were bad enough that I ended up hunting by myself, my father electing to sit this one out for more tolerable weather. Even though I got off to an early start, fresh deer sign was nearly non-existent. For reasons known only to the local deer herd, rather than feeding until sun-up, the animals had obviously ceased their activities early and had long since hunkered down in their beds.

Lack of recent deer movement, combined with a little blowing snow, can really make it difficult to age deer tracks. I had no way of knowing exactly when the deer had holed up, and the wind-blown snow made it almost impossible to decipher the gender of the maker of those tracks I did encounter. In addition to the lack of fresh deer sign, the existing snow had a decidedly frozen consistency to it, making for noisy walking. As a consequence, after an hour or so of trudging around, my initial optimism for the day had dissipated considerably. I wasn't giving up mind you; I had simply been forced to acknowledge that the odds of success were rather low.

After checking all the nearby travel corridors for deer sign, I began a larger swing of the area in an attempt to find a buck to hunt. Finally, around noon, I found a track large enough that I could be sure it belonged to a buck. This track wasn't any fresher than any of the others I had come upon to that point, but I was confident of two important things: I could at least get the buck on his feet before day's end and I could keep it separate from the other deer in the area. By my estimation, the deer I was now pursuing would weigh between 170-180 pounds once field dressed, assuming I was lucky enough to tag him. That particular outcome was merely a hope at this stage, with the odds resting clearly with the yet unseen buck.

As I set off on the track I did so at a brisk pace. Half the day was already gone and I had no idea how far I would need to travel before I arrived at the buck's hiding spot. Besides, the sign in the immediate area didn't indicate the buck was looking to bed or that he was feeding heavily, leading me to believe caution wasn't warranted.

After less than a mile of tracking, the buck's track mixed with a bunch of smaller deer in a patch of softwoods. Although I had no interest in the does and fawns, some of those tracks were quite fresh and that was a welcome change. Apparently, I had discovered the shelter-de-jour for the local deer herd.

Sensing an impending opportunity, I slowed my pace somewhat. Shortly thereafter, I came across the big buck's bed—vacant with bounding tracks heading off the hill where he had been stationed for several hours. Apparently, I hadn't slowed down sufficiently, as I neither heard nor saw the buck exit his hiding place.

Although the small deer were nowhere to be seen, I did notice that another respectable but smaller buck was now accompanying the one I had been tracking. That was fine with me; I figured I now had two deer with horns in front of me, potentially doubling my chances of getting a shot at one of them before day's end.

The two bucks started down off the knob they had been resting on all day, heading north. Once they hit a small patch of wet ground at the bottom of the hill, they turned east toward another small rise dominated by a stand of hardwoods. Before the bucks could access the deciduous trees, however, they had to traverse a very dense belt of small hemlock trees, not unlike the thick conifers I had encountered on the aforementioned hunt in New Hampshire. This time, recalling that previous set-up, I proceeded cautiously. Instead of forcing my way through the tangle and stumbling into the open, I stopped and thoroughly scanned the hardwoods while still concealed by the hemlocks.

As is so often the case when tracking deer, success and failure are separated by the smallest of things. In this instance, in a sea of mostly middle-aged deciduous trees and underbrush, I was able to identify the lower half of one stationary front leg amongst all the other vertical structure present. That's a pretty small distinction to pick up on.

In this case, however, it proved to be an essential one. I now knew the exact location of one of the bucks and, fortunately, he was within shooting range. Once I recognized the leg I was able to complete the outline of most of the rest of the buck, which was facing more or less in my direction, ready to bolt at the slightest provocation.

Instinctively, my gun snapped to my shoulder. As soon as I felt I had enough of a target to place my slug somewhere vital, I pulled the trigger. The buck immediately whirled to the left, bounding through the hardwoods and down the hill to my left at high speed. I was able to shoot a second time, but I was sure that slug missed its target.

Once I composed myself and reloaded my shotgun, I worked my way over to where the buck had been standing at my first shot. I immediately noticed a decent amount of blood, but neither the quantity nor the pattern indicated a hit to the heart or lungs. Nevertheless, I figured the deer was hit pretty hard and I would eventually claim him. After all, it was only 1pm and I had plenty of daylight left.

The buck headed northwesterly, downhill off the knob of hardwoods and across an adjacent power line. As I followed the track, I continued to see blood, but I was increasingly puzzled as to its origin. I expected the buck would take refuge and bed in the mixed cover on the far side of the power right-of-way, so I slowed to a crawl once I re-entered the woods. Even so, I continued to be disturbed by the noisiness of the snow. It was impossible to walk quietly; each step was accompanied by a loud crunching sound.

Less than 100 yards into the woods, I was pleasantly surprised to see the buck stand up about 70 yards in front of me. Facing to my right, he never even looked my way! To this day, I'm still not sure why. I couldn't imagine that he hadn't heard my approach, but perhaps he was unable to identify the direction from which the sound had emanated.

As soon as I saw the buck I had my gun up, ready to shoot. However, all I had to aim at was the buck's head and the back half of him. The heart and lungs were covered by a large tree. I quickly opted for the latter target, hoping to place the slug as far forward as possible without hitting the tree. I knew one more bullet would finish the buck, even if it wasn't immediately.

When the shotgun discharged this time, the buck ran off in the direction he was facing and quickly disappeared. Once I examined the available evidence, it was clear that this slug had struck the liver, as dark blood was copiously present. That finding made me feel better. Still uncertain about the long-term effects of my first shot, I knew an animal with a hole in its liver would not—could not—go very far.

I had only followed the tracks another 100 yards when I spied the buck lying on his side. As I approached, however, it looked like he had every intention of getting back on his feet. Only ten yards away, I sent another slug into the prostrate buck. He managed to get up anyway, and then run another 50 yards before stopping. In obvious distress, I watched the deer stand next to a large maple tree for a few seconds before finally falling over and expiring.

After this series of events I found myself emotionally exhausted but thankful that the buck was finally down. He had a heavy and symmetrical 8-point rack, and he was every bit as big as I had estimated when I first cut his track. It's worth noting that only about an hour and a half had passed since I initially discovered that track, proving that luck can change on a dime in the whitetail woods, even when conditions are far from ideal.

I made my peace with the dead buck and then got to work. Once I completed the field-dressing chores, I contemplated my options for getting the buck out of the woods. The shortest drag would only entail a half mile, but it was significantly uphill and would take me away from where my truck was parked. If I went in the opposite direction, the terrain was level to slightly downhill and my truck would be there. Of course, the downside of this plan was a much longer drag—at least a mile.

I chose the second option, but I still figured I'd be home well before dark. As it turned out, I didn't arrive at my truck until the sun was setting. By then, I was exhausted, dehydrated and slightly hypothermic. I was able to muscle the deer into the bed of my truck by backing up to a small incline, using it to lift the buck to the same height as the tailgate. If that rise hadn't been there, I don't know what I would have done, as my efforts to lift the buck directly off the ground and into truck had been unsuccessful.

I stopped at the local store to show the buck to its proprietor and sometime hunting companion, Ken Estes. The visit also served a more urgent purpose: to pour some much-needed liquid into my system. By this time, I was noticeably shaking from the combined effects of my exertion and the day-long lack of water.

Refreshed somewhat, I drove to the local deer checking station, where the buck was aged at $3^1/_2$ years. He tipped the scales at 174 pounds, just as I had originally surmised. Once home, my wife and kids were thrilled to see me, and we reveled in my success.

Without my earlier experience with that buck in New Hampshire, this day most likely would have turned out quite different. We all make mistakes; they're unavoidable. As long as we learn from our errors, making them one-time events, the prospect for future success is only enhanced.

One last thing: I hate mysteries, so I was understandably curious about the damage my first shot had caused. Despite my best efforts, I was never able to come to a definite conclusion. As best as I could tell, the slug entered the deer's armpit but didn't breach the rib cage. My analysis was hindered by the path of my final shot, which traversed the same anatomy (more or less) but in the opposite direction.

The New Hampshire gang in 1969 with a black bear my father killed. Back row, left to right: Al Cady, Billy Drew, Art Morey and a very young author. Front row, left to right: Bob Donnelly, bruin and Charles Carter.

Photo by Hazen Morey

Spent shotgun shell casing, Fish & Game metal seal and slugs taken from the buck.

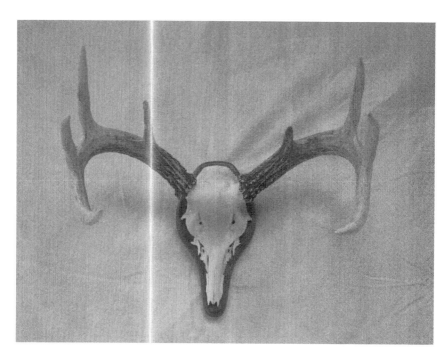

After learning a valuable lesson while hunting in New Hampshire, I used the knowledge to help me kill this heavy-horned 8-point buck in Massachusetts. The mount is one of my own concoctions. After removing soft tissue, I carefully saw through the skull from back to front, leaving the antlers attached to a substantial bony base. I then mount the skull plate to an oak plaque that is slightly larger than the outline of the bony structure.

Serendipitous Snow

The 2005 shotgun season had already been a successful one, as I had been fortunate to shoot a young buck during the first week. As the second week drew to a close, however, I was thinking less about hunting deer and more about my impending trip to Mexico. I was about to embark on a long-anticipated hunt for desert bighorn sheep. At the time, a sheep hunt was the only thing within my control that could conceivably relegate deer hunting to a subordinate place on my list of things to do. Despite my best efforts, I was unable to schedule the trip south of the border so that it wouldn't coincide with my deer hunting. Consequently, the deer were about to get a break, at least from me.

I was scheduled to leave for Mexico on Sunday. Not wanting to be too hurried in my preparations, thus causing me to forget some crucial item, I planned to use the preceding Saturday to finalize my packing and see to any last-minute arrangements. However, it unexpectedly snowed late Friday night. When I awoke early Saturday morning, the ground was covered with a foot of dry, powdery snow. From a tracker's perspective, an event like this can only be described as momentous—a meteorological gift of great magnitude.

Theoretically, tracking can be employed anytime there's enough snow on the ground to see the imprint of a hoof. Deer can even be followed on bare ground when the conditions are perfect, such as when trailing a huge buck in the immediate aftermath of a heavy, leaf-flattening rain. In the real world, however, tracking is often an impractical means of killing a deer, at least while hunting solo. Being able to pick up a track and shooting the deer which made it are not equivalent events. Before a deer can be killed, the hunter must be able to approach to within some reasonable shooting distance.

And that's where the quality of the snow comes into play. While it's certainly possible to have too much or too little of the white stuff, more than anything else, it's the amount of noise that's produced when stepping in snow that most often dictates how approachable deer are. Snow conditions not particularly conducive to tracking include: a top layer exhibiting an icy crust, a general frozen consistency and moisture-laden snow, which is prone to excessive "squeaking" when subjected to compression. Naturally, the condition of the underlying soil plays a role, as well. There are countless combinations of snow depth, snow quality and soil condition which ultimately determine how quietly one can walk in the woods.

In the final analysis, though, I can say this with some confidence: On average, for every thirty-odd-day hunting season where I live, there may be only five days when it's even possible to kill a deer while tracking. Of those five days, no more than two would be considered ideal days to track. Of course, there is wide year-to-year fluctuation in conditions. During some hunting seasons snow is almost completely absent; in others, snow is present, in one form or another, the entire time.

I make this small digression as a means of underscoring just how enticing the snow conditions were on that Saturday morn. In my view, it just didn't get much better than that. So, I decided to forestall my trip preparations and go hunting. First, I called hunting partner John Dupuis to notify him of my change of heart. We both had to rid our driveways of the unanticipated but welcome white blanket, so the hunt wouldn't start immediately. Since my truck was equipped with a plow, I offered to be the day's designated driver. The extra equipment would enable me to carve out a parking spot on the road's shoulder.

With our driveways navigable, John and I headed to a spot we had reason to believe held some deer. We entered the woods before 9am, John choosing one route while I made a swing along a different path. The immediate object was to find tracks so we could narrow down our options somewhat. There was no way of telling where the deer had been at the onset of the storm, but we fully expected to find fresh sign somewhere, especially given the storm's cessation just before dawn.

The going wasn't easy but it wasn't horrible either. If the snow had been wet and heavy, walking would have been exhausting work. As things were, the light and fluffy consistency allowed me to swing my legs through the sea of white, rather than lifting each leg out of its posthole before stepping anew. Still, my progress wasn't nearly as fast as I would have liked, and I was generating slightly more body heat than I needed to stay warm.

After a half mile or so, I intercepted some fresh feeding sign near a stand of apple trees. One of these tracks had been made by a brute of a buck. The conditions wouldn't allow for a close examination of the imprint of the buck's hoof, as loose snow would fall back into the twelve-inch-deep indentation. Nevertheless, I pegged the buck at 170-180 pounds (field-dressed weight) based solely on the size of the slot made in the snow.

The deep, loose snow posed other problems related to reading deer sign. Simply determining the direction in which a deer was walking required concentration and attention to detail. Under most other circumstances, the deer's toes could be used to point the way forward, but they weren't discernible in the current snow conditions. I was forced to rely on secondary indicators to reveal the deer's direction of travel, such as the back-to-front sweep of a leg with its attendant drag marks and snow deposits forward of the track.

After sorting the entirety of the sign in the vicinity of the apple trees, I ultimately concluded that several deer were traveling together, and they were headed up the hill to a more remote section of woods. Once the deer coalesced along a nearly single path, I was only intermittently able to identify the big buck's track among all the others. In fact, for stretches of 100 yards or more at a time, I would have defied anyone to prove a buck of this magnitude had passed by.

From all appearances, the trail looked like it had been made by an average group of does and fawns. However, I knew the big deer was there, and the sign indicated something else: the buck had preceded the other deer up the mountain. That's why there was so little evidence of his passing. Each successive deer had, in turn, obliterated more evidence of the buck's existence as they advanced in a nearly single-file procession.

After crossing a couple of smallish brooks, the herd slowly made its way west, headed higher all the time. At one point, about an hour into the effort, I noticed where the buck had stopped to rub a tree. If nothing else, the fresh shavings of bark, now melting into the top layer of snow, bore witness to the fact that the buck was still wearing his antlers. Shortly thereafter, the small herd turned to the north, continuing to ascend along the crest of a finger ridge.

I had been looking for the deer for some time as I slowly trailed behind. With this much snow on the ground, I knew I would have to adjust my expectations regarding what portion of a deer might be visible, especially if I encountered the deer in their beds. In that case, I would be lucky to see anything more than an animal's head. The remainder of the form would undoubtedly be enveloped within a veritable bathtub in the snow, making it impossible to identify legs or even the outline of a deer's body.

There were open hardwoods to my left. For some reason, my intuitive sixth sense told me I was more likely to catch sight of the deer there instead of to my front, where the tracks were leading me. In large part, this was a conditioned response forged by my prior experiences, where only rarely were deer found directly in line with the tracks. Most of the time, deer I tracked were eventually seen to the left or the right of the spoor, but almost never straight ahead.

I had long ago learned to trust my gut, but this time my instincts failed me. Even so, if I had been moving a little slower and more cautiously, I still might have prevailed. I was swinging my eyes in all directions in search of the deer, but I was concentrating more on the hardwoods to my left. As my focus drifted back to the right, I locked eyes with a bedded buck a mere sixty yards up the hill.

I'm sure the buck had been watching me for a second or two before I happened to discover him. The bedded deer had the jump on me and before I could bring my gun to my shoulder, the buck bolted from his bed, leaving a snowy micro-blizzard in his wake. In a split second, the deer was gone from sight.

Once things settled back down, I scolded myself for my errors. The buck had been positioned on a small plateau dominated by hemlocks. Upon reflection, I was forced to concede that the hemlocks provided a more likely resting spot than did the hardwoods. More important than my misguided instinct was my failure to thoroughly scan all conceivable locations for sign of deer, while standing still and before taking my next step. In sum, I just hadn't been careful enough and a perfectly good opportunity was lost, at least for the time being.

As I stood in place, digesting what had just happened, I had some additional thoughts, all of which were completely unrelated to my recent performance. During my brief look at the bedded buck I was only able to see his head, as the rest of the deer's body was in a deep snowy depression. This much I had anticipated. I easily noticed the buck's antlers, which appeared to be rather narrow of spread and weak of mass for a deer I expected to weigh in excess of 170 pounds. That was surprising.

In my mind, the most likely explanation was that the group I had trailed to this place contained a second, smaller buck. If so, that meant I hadn't yet seen the big buck I was really after. I also considered the possibility that I had misjudged the buck's track, and the buck which I had observed was, indeed, the only buck in the group. He just wasn't as big as I had estimated from the spoor. I dismissed this prospect rather quickly; I knew what I had seen, and the track was far above average.

None of this speculation really mattered. I had proof positive that at least one buck had been nearby. At this point, I needed to unravel whatever sign was available and get back on track, literally. I started my search in the clump of hemlocks, where I found four beds in total. Other than the bounding tracks which exited these beds, no other deer had walked beyond this place. Three of the deer headed north together, while the fourth, the deer I had seen, ran off in a more easterly direction.

Most telling was the fact that there were no oversize tracks among the three animals heading north, either in the beds or along their exit route. On the other hand, the buck I had seen occupied the largest bed of the four, and his running track was decidedly more impressive than the others.

That this deer seemed to shun the other three was helpful on several fronts. First, it simplified the amount of sign I would have to evaluate. Second, it served to confirm that I had singled out the best—and most likely only—buck in the bunch. Finally, my chances of getting a legitimate shooting opportunity would be enhanced, now that the buck was by himself. I would only have to overcome one deer's senses instead of those of all four animals.

All this compiling and sifting of information took some time, as I made repeated circles in the area of the hemlocks. Conditions were far from ideal and judgments had to be made on subtle distinctions instead of obvious differences. I was careful not to miss something important that would have altered my final conclusion, such as the presence of a fifth deer.

Confident that I had successfully sorted the available sign, I resumed the tracking effort. It wasn't long before the running track I was following swung to the south, parallel to and just east of the ridge the deer had been bedded on. I hadn't gone 200 yards when I identified the hindquarters of a standing deer less than 100 yards below me. The buck was facing almost directly away, with his head turned back in my direction.

I came to a screeching stop, and I didn't wait for a more favorable presentation. I quickly aimed at the left side of the deer's rump and fired the shotgun. I was hopeful that my slug would make it to the vitals, despite the animal's steeply angled presentation. At the very least, I knew that the buck would be crippled, assuming my aim had been true and my execution flawless.

I hurried down to where the buck had been standing and discovered heavy blood sign. Obviously, my slug had found its mark and I was optimistic that the deer would shortly be mine. As I followed the buck, all the bleeding seemed to be concentrated on the left side of the trail.

I had slowly advanced along the deer's path of retreat another 100 yards, when I suddenly noticed the buck standing in front of me, barely fifty yards away. I had him dead to rights, but my gun didn't fire when I pulled the trigger. I had most likely "short-stroked" the pump action subsequent to shooting the first time, and the result was that the firing pin fell on an empty chamber.

Naturally, the buck didn't stand around waiting for me to fix my gun; he hurriedly limped away. Once the shotgun was back in working order, I renewed my careful stalk. There was a copious amount of blood where the buck had stood, and his left hind leg didn't appear to be of much use. I was certain that the deer's suffering would be soon over. After all, if the buck had let me approach to within rock-throwing distance once, he could be expected to do so again.

A few seconds later, I had one more opportunity to end the deer's life as he thrashed awkwardly through a thicket. Unfortunately, my slug center-punched a small tree. Moments after that, I was able to close to within ten yards and shoot the now-prostrate buck in the lungs, ending the deer's troubles. All told, from first shot to last, not ten minutes had passed. I could finally relax and enjoy the fruits of my labor.

The buck looked pretty big, but he was still very much buried in snow. Thus, I found myself somewhat ambivalent about assigning the deer an estimated field-dressed weight. The buck's antlers were no more impressive up close than they had been when viewed from a distance. The rack was narrow and rather spindly, consistent with my initial take. For some reason, the buck never grew brow tines, which officially made him a six-pointer. The antlers seemed more typical of those found on a $2^{1}/_{2}$-year-old. With the exception of providing feedback regarding how accurate my reading of sign had been, none of these physical traits really mattered to me. They were mere items of curiosity. I was thrilled to have taken this buck.

I unloaded my shotgun, removed my coat and got to work. By the time I was ready to start pulling on the deer, it wasn't quite noon. I couldn't help but think that the outcome was pretty special, especially considering I hadn't even planned to go hunting on this day. I was more than two miles from my truck, and I had no idea where John had ended up. With the heavy snow hanging on the trees, I wasn't even sure that he had heard me shooting. Before moving the deer, I decided to do a little reconnaissance as a means of selecting the best path out of the woods.

When tracking deer, my attention is focused primarily on the animal in front of me and only secondarily on where I am at any given time. Though this practice rarely results in a feeling of truly being lost, it does frequently cause some temporary disorientation. The presence of heavy snow can add to the effect, because landmarks aren't as recognizable as usually. This day happened to feature both of the aforementioned elements. And so, as I searched for an acceptable exit route, I was pleasantly surprised to find a private driveway less than 200 yards to the south.

I now knew exactly where I was. The drag wasn't going to be nearly as difficult as I had envisioned just moments before. I hauled the buck a little closer to the road, leaving the deer and my shotgun in an out-of-the-way spot. Rather than plowing through heavy snow to reach my truck, I decided to return via the available road system. This would add about a mile to my journey, but I figured this approach would be quicker and less tiring than slogging through the snow-laden woods.

Less than an hour later I returned and picked up my trophy. I noticed an interesting thing: Once I had the buck out of the snow and into the open, he seemed to get bigger. At long last, any doubts I may have harbored regarding the buck's weight were fading. I now felt confident that the deer would break the 170-pound threshold I had originally set for him when I first spied his track. The definitive answer would come at my next stop, the local checking station.

Given the perfect hunting conditions, I was surprised to find no other hunters at the state-run facility. The attendant cheerfully examined the buck. A quick check of the deer's teeth revealed him to be $3^{1}/_{2}$ years old. When we threw the buck on the scales he weighed 174 pounds, validating my earliest estimate. I take great pride in my ability to read deer sign, so this information bolstered my sense of satisfaction with the day's effort. Since no one else pulled up, the attendant and I continued our conversation for several minutes before I finally left.

I made a short side trip to my parents' house, to share my success, before returning home. After hanging the buck in my garage and eating some lunch, I went to check on John. I didn't want my companion to think I left him high and dry. John was still in the woods and I didn't want to interrupt his hunt, so I periodically drove the road throughout the afternoon. We finally reconnected around 3pm. I told John my tale and took him to the house to show him the deer. John was pretty tired from all the walking he had done, so my wife offered him refreshments before I brought my friend home.

In the days that followed this hunt, as I contemplated my good fortune, I couldn't help but wonder why the buck had behaved the way he did. Specifically, I had jumped the buck from his bed when he saw me approaching up the ridge. Yet, in spite of this scare he only ran 200 yards before stopping. In my experience, such behavior is quite rare. In all probability, the explanation is related to the snow depth. The buck just didn't want to exert himself any more than absolutely necessary.

It's also true that I spent approximately twenty minutes sorting through sign in the area of the hemlock stand. When the buck wasn't immediately pursued, that may have bolstered his expectation that I had passed on by and he wouldn't need to flee any further. Once I resumed the track,

I was able to walk very quietly and visibility was poor, reducing the buck's ability to detect me. Plus, when I recognized the standing deer I was still 100 yards away from him. One more step on my part would have likely put the buck to flight once again.

In any event, I was fortunate to see the buck when I did, and the buck paid for his miscalculations with his life. I've always said, "If the deer don't make any mistakes, you can't kill them."

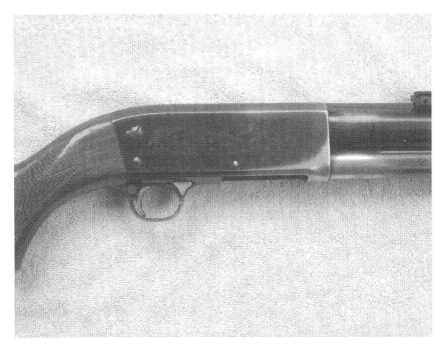

The well-worn Ithaca 12-gauge shotgun I used to kill the buck in this story. I killed many deer with this gun over the years, but I've recently replaced it.

Here I'm walking in powdery snow, although it's not quite as deep as what I experienced in the hunt central to this chapter. Just telling a deer's direction of travel can be challenging in conditions such as these.

Photo by Janet Carter

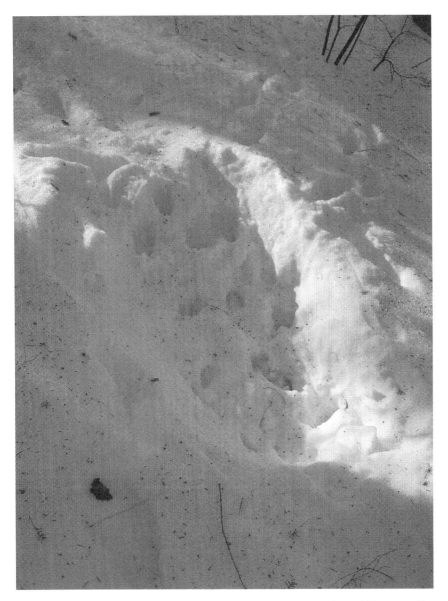

A deer bed in deep snow. For all intents and purposes, it's shaped like a small oval bathtub. When looking for a bedded deer in such circumstances, all you can usually see is the deer's head.

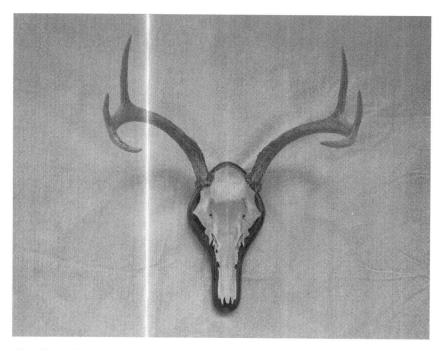

The "Serendipitous Snow" buck. Although the antlers are somewhat spindly for a 3½-year-old animal, the buck still weighed 174 pounds.

WHAT IN THE WORLD DO
I HAVE TO DO?

Not every hunt has all the pieces fall into place as nicely as they did in the preceding story. For every such tale, there seems to be at least one hunt that serves as a counter-balance to that rare occasion when the stars are all in alignment. And, it's frequently the case that when luck turns, it can move a long way in the opposite direction. While no one expects to kill a deer every time he or she steps into the woods, sometimes events can play out in a particularly confounding manner—one that leaves you scratching your head or, perhaps even, pulling out your hair.

The year was 2003 or 2004, I'm not sure which. Both hunting seasons proved equally troublesome, at least for me. During the shotgun season of the year in question, I had hunted an area and discovered two huge rubbed trees within a few hundred yards of each other. One of these specimens measured a whopping nine inches in diameter, while the other was even bigger—exceeding twelve inches! To this very day, those trees comprise the two biggest rubs I've ever encountered. Obviously, at least one good buck considered this section of woods home.

With one day left in the entire season, a fresh two-inch snowfall lured me back to this place in one last attempt to find the maker of these gargantuan rubs. Of course, it was a distinct possibility that another hunter had long ago tagged the buck responsible for shredding the trees. I first needed to find a big track before I could hunt a big deer. I felt my best opportunity to cut such sign could be found via a wood road which divided the larger area.

I parked my truck at the southern entry point to the skid trail and quickly headed down the break in search of tracks. About a mile into my journey I found what I had been seeking. Actually, my cup runneth over, so to speak. In total, five deer had crossed the path in the same place, headed east. More important, two of the deer were big bucks. I estimated both would weigh in excess of 170 pounds, assuming I could get one of them on the ground.

Despite their supposed similarity in body size, the tracks indicated that the hooves of the bucks were shaped differently. One track was typical of a deer this size, exhibiting well-rounded toes and a heart-shaped outline exceeding two inches in width. The second track, although just as wide, was longer and it featured pointed toes.

The sign was fairly recent and all five deer were slowly working their way through the hardwoods and down a significant hill. As I followed along, the temperature was steadily climbing. Nearly a mile from where I had originally intercepted the tracks, the deer approached an area that seemed to be a likely place for them to bed.

This location was at the top of a steep drop-off, and it was dominated by softwoods. I slowed down considerably in anticipation of stalking bedded deer. However, I hadn't yet entered the belt of conifers when I noticed two running tracks headed southwest. And those tracks just happened to belong to the two big bucks.

I didn't bother to sort out all the sign in the area, so I would never know whether the deer had actually bedded nearby. Neither did I come to understand why the bucks had so hurriedly fled. I suppose an errant breeze had prematurely alerted the deer to my presence, but who really knows? In all honesty, I could have cared less what spooked the deer to begin with, why the group suddenly split up and where the other three deer had gone. I had the two deer I was most interested in, fresh in front of me, with more than half the day still available to hunt them.

On their present course, the bucks were headed back in the general direction of my parked vehicle, but slightly to the south. That suited me fine. It was a long, slow slog back up the hill, but the deer finally stopped running, slowing to a steady walk by the time I reached the top. When the bucks subsequently crossed a nearby unimproved road, I had a pretty good idea where I'd find them.

The bucks had entered another block of woods dominated by spruce and balsam fir. I knew from years of experience that deer preferred to bed on this particular hill. The bucks had traveled at least a mile; their behavior was now relaxed; and they had just crossed into a known bedding area. So as soon as I set foot in this parcel of land, I immediately went into stealth mode. I fully expected to encounter the deer at any moment.

The current temperature was approaching 40° Fahrenheit, making for quiet stalking in the rapidly melting snow. I carefully picked my way through the forest, searching from side to side for any sign of the bucks as I advanced. The tracks had begun to meander slightly, another indication that bedding was imminent. As I slipped around a large yellow birch tree, I suddenly noticed one of the bucks lying to my right, a scant sixty yards from where I was standing.

The first thing I did was to check the wind, so I would have some sense as to how much time was available to consider my options. Satisfied that the direction was favorable and likely to remain so, I took a better look with my binoculars. The buck seemed completely relaxed and totally unaware of my presence. For the time being, he was looking down the hill and away from me. My heart sank, though, when I realized the bedded buck was missing both antlers! I figured the second buck was almost certainly nearby, but I couldn't see him from my current location. I could only hope that the unseen buck still carried his headgear.

It was now about 2pm. I had barely released the grip on my binoculars when the buck suddenly turned and stared in my direction. From his standpoint, I'm sure something didn't look right because he maintained this alert pose for a full ten minutes. I was completely stationary and my outline was screened by some intervening brush, but I was still pretty much out in the open. I knew that the slightest movement would completely blow whatever chances I had left.

To my great relief, the buck finally turned his head away. A few minutes later, though, he abruptly swung his head back in my direction. The deer maintained his gaze for several more minutes before once again resuming a more relaxed posture. This sequence happened several times, but the number of minutes the buck spent looking my way decreased with each successive cycle. Eventually, the bedded buck abandoned these checks, apparently satisfied that I was just part of the landscape and no danger was lurking in my direction.

Based upon the first deer's location and his body position, I had a pretty good idea where the second buck was hiding out. I figured he was bedded higher on the hill and to the left of the first buck, probably no more than twenty yards away from his partner. Based upon the terrain and the first buck's orientation, I also assumed he was facing my way. Unfortunately for me, trees and brush completely blocked my view of that section of the hill. Moreover, I dared not move because the antlerless buck was already suspicious and any motion on my part would probably be noticed.

Even if I hadn't been concerned about the first buck detecting me, I still faced obstacles. With my next step forward, I would have popped out from behind a large tree and presumably into view of the second buck. I also had snow behind me, which would tend to make any motion on my part more conspicuous.

On the other hand, the hillside the buck occupied was a mottling of brown and white, mostly brown. If the deer was bedded on bare ground, which was a distinct possibility, it might take me a few seconds to find him. Given the most likely scenario, it would have been almost impossible for me to isolate the buck, confirm he still had antlers, aim and shoot before the second deer ran out of sight. I was in a difficult situation and I knew it.

After thinking through all my options, I decided my best bet was to stay in place and hope the deer got up to feed before it became too dark to shoot. Fortunately, the temperature allowed for this possibility, as it was unusually warm for the last day of December. If it had been twenty degrees colder, I would have found myself in a bit of a predicament. And so, I hunkered in place for what could prove to be a very long time. I waited and watched, and waited some more, ever vigilant to a change in circumstances. Two excruciatingly long hours later, there was still no indication that the bucks were about to stir.

Despite the competing senses of anticipation and frustration that consumed me during this period, I must acknowledge how unique the experience was. I've been in the presence of bedded deer before and since this episode, but never for this extraordinary length of time. To be honest, I enjoyed watching the lone visible buck and I felt privileged to be a party to the natural world. Obviously, had he still been in possession of his headgear, I would have derived even more satisfaction from shooting the buck in his bed at the earliest opportunity. Nonetheless, I couldn't help but feel good about the hunting skills which had allowed me to sneak to within sixty yards of two mature bucks, and remain undetected for all this time.

Time was growing short and when my watch struck 4pm, I started to seriously consider what cards I had left to play. Darkness was descending, and it wouldn't be long before I would be unable to see the iron sights on my muzzleloader. With the deer apparently wholly content with the status quo, I decided I had to push the issue if I was to have any chance at all. After examining the possibilities, I elected to try sneaking a few steps toward the buck which was within sight. If I could do so without being noticed, I hoped my new vantage point would expose the hidden buck's location.

By carefully advancing in slow motion and by using the few available trees to partially screen my movements, I was able to advance about five yards. Still, I couldn't will the second buck into focus. Another fifteen minutes worth of valuable sand had slipped to the bottom half of the hourglass. As I attempted to further improve my position, I apparently made a mistake. I don't recall whether I snapped a twig or one of the bucks caught sight of me in the process of moving, but both deer suddenly came to full alert, simultaneously jumping to their feet.

At long last, I finally had a chance to lay eyes on the long-hidden buck, but only briefly. He had been bedded almost exactly where I had imagined. Between the impending darkness and the mostly snow-less background, I still had trouble picking out his outline. Before I could get my gun to my shoulder, both bucks were on the move. The second buck was two jumps from the crest of the hill, where he would be completely safe. Although I managed to bring my muzzleloader to bear, I couldn't see enough of my sights or the running buck to justify pulling the trigger. There was one item I could positively identify in the deepening gloom—the buck's still-attached antlers as he crested the ridge and disappeared!

Of course, my brief glimpse of the buck's rack only served to magnify my profound sense of disappointment. Antlers or not, the hunting season was over! I stumbled back to the dirt road and walked that route the remaining mile to my truck, shaking my head the whole way. It was completely dark by the time I arrived.

As I reflected on the afternoon's events on the way home, there was a certain dichotomy that lingered over the day. The experience contained equal parts of excitement and depression. It seemed like I should have killed the antlered buck, yet had I done so I would have called the feat a near miracle. I found myself unwilling to laugh at the outcome and unable to cry over my bad luck. In fact, the whole episode was so unusual, it almost seemed as though it had never happened at all.

As more time passed, my mind naturally drifted to the "what ifs." The first and most obvious such inquiry was: What if the antlered buck had been lying in the bald buck's spot? And that's just another way of pleading, "Why didn't the buck I could see have horns?" Of course, there could be no satisfactory answer to that question. The situation was what it was. The forces governing antler shedding and the selection of bedding sites aren't entirely knowable and predictable, and they certainly aren't designed with the best interests of hunters in mind. Sometimes we're left to ponder the imponderables.

Of those things over which I did have control, however, I constantly replayed the events of that day, as I tried to evaluate whether an alternative course of action would have produced a different—more favorable—outcome. I contemplated the possible effects of using a grunt vocalization to rouse the bucks, as well as starting my move on the deer slightly earlier than I had.

Hindsight has its place, if it's used to learn from mistakes and make improvements. However, second-guesses can neither be proved correct nor dismissed as failures. In the final analysis, all of us are forced to do the best we can in whatever circumstances we find ourselves. And sometimes, no matter how hard we try or how much we get right, each of us is left to wonder: What in the world do I have to do?

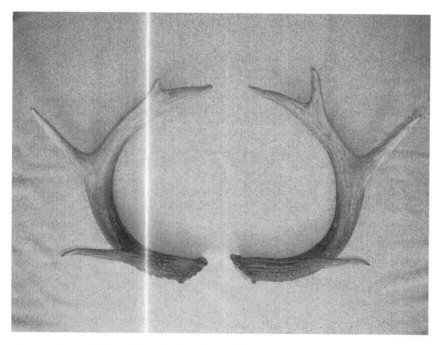

A very nice set of matching shed antlers. They don't belong to either of the bucks which were central to this story.

This is an impressive rub on a hard maple tree measuring seven inches in diameter. However, the rubs I found in the area where the two big bucks in the story resided involved trees even bigger: nine and twelve inches!

This is the muzzleloader I used on the hunt featured in this chapter. The peep sight certainly limited my ability to shoot as darkness descended.

ANTLERS, AT LAST

I was lucky enough to draw a coveted either-sex permit for the 1981 hunting season. I'm pretty sure it wasn't my first, and it definitely wouldn't be my last. I guess I've had more than my fair share over the years. On a couple of different occasions, my father and I have both drawn in the same year. Go figure. At that time, a hunter could only kill one deer per year, and the single biggest advantage these permits offered was that the holder wasn't required to identify antlers before shooting at a deer. That is, unless that hunter only wanted to kill bucks. As deer became more plentiful and hunting seasons and bag limits were made more liberal, the permit system evolved somewhat.

At that point in my life, I only had a single deer to my credit, so I was much more interested in doubling my production than in hunting horns. It was on the second day of the December shotgun season that I was able to put my doe permit to use, but not entirely in the manner I had expected. I was hunting in Windsor with Kenny Estes, his brother Richard and Billy Drew. The day featured moderate temperatures, as well as enough snow to cover the ground and weigh down the boughs of the plentiful balsam fir trees in the area. In fact, the woods were quite beautiful.

Our first effort that morning involved a push through a smallish section of woods that we were all familiar with. Two members of the group took roles as standers, while the other two walked through the cover. I was one of the walkers. The hunt was expected to last about an hour. If nothing turned up we would regroup, pile back into the vehicles, and then move somewhere else in hopes of better hunting.

I worked my way back and forth through my appointed travel corridor without finding any fresh deer sign. A stone wall marked the end of the effort, and it was there that I met up with Ken, who was standing near an old blowdown. We carried on a quiet conversation while we waited for the others to join us. I was facing Ken and he was looking back in the direction from which I had just come.

As we spoke, I suddenly noticed Ken's eyes getting bigger as he craned his neck. Figuring something was up, I turned to see what had so abruptly grabbed Kenny's attention. Slinking through the cover were a doe and two fawns. Where they had come from, I didn't have a clue. On my passage over the same ground only five minutes earlier, there hadn't been a hint of their existence.

Apparently, I could see the deer better and over a longer span of time than could Ken, because I was able to shoot five times and he only fired once. It wasn't like the deer were walking in the open. There was plenty of brush and numerous trees shielding the animals. Plus, after the first shot the whole situation turned rather chaotic. Once the deer disappeared, a thorough search of the area revealed blood associated with the doe's track.

I must admit, especially when judged against my current standards and skills, my performance had been pretty pathetic. In large part, my inexperience could be blamed. However, another factor played a prominent role in my poor marksmanship. My first shot and at least one of the subsequent rounds had utilized buckshot instead of slugs. Back then, buckshot was commonly used by the people I hunted with, and I willingly followed their lead.

However, this day would prove to be the last time I would load such ammunition in my shotgun. Wounding animals is something that really bothers me, as I've done my share. Over the years, I've seen too many deer which were struck with a single pellet of buckshot, often outside the vitals. Some animals were recovered, many more weren't. In the vast majority of cases, the blood trail could be described as marginal to non-existent, especially on bare ground.

I'm not crusading to have buckshot outlawed and I respect everyone's right of individual choice in this matter. I readily admit that, in the right person's hands, buckshot is every bit as effective as a slug. However, when compared to slugs, I do believe the use of buckshot poses an unnecessarily high risk of wounding game, as well as an unacceptably low probability of subsequently recovering a wounded animal. I'd rather shoot slugs.

The blood sign the doe was leaving was skimpy at best, and more indicative of a wound not involving the vitals. Kenny hadn't fired at the doe, so she must have been hit by me. After feeding another five shells into my Ithaca twelve-gauge, I set off on the doe's track in hopes of finishing her off. The fawns had scattered elsewhere in the mayhem, so I had a single deer in front of me.

After following the track for a while, I thought I had a better understanding regarding the anatomical location of the doe's wound. The process of elimination I employed went something like this: No bones seemed to be broken, as her gait was completely normal. The doe hadn't been hit in the heart or lungs, or she would have surely died by this time. Neither had the deer been gut shot, as there was no stomach matter to be found. As best as I could tell, a single piece of buckshot had hit the doe. The most likely place, based upon the location of the blood droplets, was in a muscle of one of her hind legs.

I followed the doe over hill and dale for the rest of the morning and into the afternoon. I jumped her out of her bed a couple of times, and I even caught sight of her once. Despite the fact that I had a pretty good look at the deer, I just couldn't quite put the gun on her before she disappeared. By this time, the bleeding had slowed to an occasional drop every five yards or so. Based upon this evidence and the doe's general demeanor, I figured she would ultimately survive her wounds. Nonetheless, I opted to stay on the doe's trail the rest of the day, still hopeful that I'd eventually be able to put my tag on her.

To this point in time, the doe had been content to stay in the same general area where I had first seen her, always staying just ahead of me. But, after a few hours of my persistent pursuit, the deer finally shifted gears and headed towards an adjoining section of woods.

About 2pm, I followed the track to the near bank of a significant drop off. A small brook coursed through the bottom, some thirty feet in elevation lower. From there, the opposite bank rose to the same level as the one where I stood. The gulf from one side to the other was considerable, spanning nearly 100 yards.

When I arrived at the embankment, I immediately looked across the divide for sign of the moving doe. The lack of eye-level vegetation allowed for more open viewing than I had experienced to this point in the day. I immediately recognized a deer on the far side, but this one had antlers growing from his head and that was an unexpected discovery. The buck seemed to be feeding, and he had no notion I was in the neighborhood.

I quickly assumed the steadiest shooting position available to me. I elevated the bead at the end of the barrel to the top of the buck's broadside back and sent a slug his way. The deer immediately disappeared from view without displaying any obvious signs that the lead projectile had found its mark. A few seconds later, a deer popped into view near where the buck had been standing, so I shot again. Subsequently, two other deer sped into and out of sight before I was tempted to pull the trigger once more. Apparently, the section of woods on the opposite bank was home to the entire deer herd of Windsor.

All of this action proved to be more than a little exasperating, but that was nothing compared to what I faced next. The doe I had been following was on the far side of the brook, plus I had taken two aimed shots at one, and perhaps a second, additional animal. With the presence of so many deer and an abundance of sign, I could look forward to a very difficult time sorting through the spoor. I took careful note of where the various animals had been standing when I fired, so I'd know where to concentrate my searches.

At this juncture, I was perfectly willing to let the doe I had been trailing go her way. As I described earlier, I was confident her wound wasn't life-threatening. Before that could happen, I needed to account for any blood I found and attribute it to a specific animal.

Once on the far bank, I started my effort where the buck had been standing, whereupon I immediately noticed a tuft of brown hair sitting on the top of the snow. I now knew that my first slug had hit pay dirt but little else, at least for the time being. This finding brightened my outlook, but I decided to check the rest of the available sign before returning to the buck's track.

After thoroughly canvassing the remainder of the hillside, I was able to conclude that the second deer I had fired on wasn't the buck I had hit with my first shot. Moreover, the second slug had thankfully missed its mark. The last thing I needed was an additional wounded deer to deal with. The doe which was responsible for bringing me to this place had apparently continued on through without stopping. Somewhat relieved that I had managed to distill the abundance of information to its essentials, I turned my attention back to the buck.

Necessarily, all this detective work consumed a great deal of time, nearly an hour. It was approaching 3pm when I started on the buck's track. There was very little bleeding accompanying the cut hair I had previously discovered, and I began to suspect that I had gut shot the deer. Fortunately, the buck pretty much kept to himself during his retreat, making it easier to isolate his track.

I had been trailing the wounded buck for approximately 100 yards, when I heard a snort. I looked up to see him bounding from his bed eighty yards to my front. I managed to fire another round before he disappeared, but that slug missed completely. Although the buck was able to run, he demonstrated a hunched-up appearance as he fled. To me, it also appeared as though the deer wasn't moving at full speed.

Before I went any further, I figured it was time to take an inventory of my remaining ammunition. After rifling through all my pockets, I realized I was down to my last two slugs, which made me more than a little nervous. I had a badly wounded buck on my hands, barely more than an hour of daylight available and only two shotgun shells left to get the job done. If I was to succeed, I would have to become much more efficient than I had been to this point in the day.

So far, my operating premise was that the first slug had punched a hole in the buck's paunch, and the presence of stomach matter in the deer's bed confirmed that result. The buck's behavior indicated he was really hurting.

Although the prudent approach might have been to leave and come back the next day, at that time in my life I was far too impatient to move that option to the top of the list. I wanted this all to be over as soon as possible. Besides, no matter what happened in the final hour of daylight, based upon what I had seen thus far, I couldn't imagine the buck traveling more than 500 additional yards before lying down and eventually succumbing to the internal damage. I figured I would either kill the buck before dark, or find him dead somewhere in the immediate vicinity in the morning.

As I trailed the buck anew I was much more cautious than I had been initially. While I hadn't quite been certain what I was dealing with prior to this juncture, I now knew the buck was grievously wounded. Less than 100 yards later, I found the deer standing behind a tree about fifty yards away.

I could see the buck's nose and hindquarters, but that was it. As I tried to figure out a way to thread the needle and get another slug into the deer, I could see the buck shaking as he stood in place. Although I tried mightily, I just couldn't get a better look without changing my location. I was afraid that the buck would run off if I took another step, so I reluctantly decided to try and put a slug into his hips. If I was successful, the buck would go down and I'd be able to run over and finish him off.

Alas, the lead missed its mark and the buck hobbled out of sight anyway. My shotgun now held but a single shell. I would have to be extremely careful how I used it, as there was no longer any margin for error. At this point, I was even seriously considering the possibility that I would ultimately have to dispatch the buck using my hunting knife. As I prepared for our next meeting, I also realized that the buck hadn't been headed in any particular direction. Instead, he was just tracing loops over a rather small area as he attempted to evade me.

I next followed the track into a patch of thigh-high evergreens. I was creeping along, intently looking for the deer. I expected to see him at a range of twenty-five to fifty yards. After all, that was how near the buck had allowed me to approach on our last encounter. Instead, I received the shock of ten lifetimes when the buck suddenly exploded out of his bed in the low spruces less than five feet away! Before I could come to my senses, the deer crested the nearby hill and was gone from sight.

It's really hard to describe just how startled I was as a result of this event. Literally, I had very nearly stepped on the wounded buck. If he had turned towards me rather than away, it was a distinct possibility that I would have been seriously injured. I could only imagine the damage that could have been inflicted upon me by those antlers, had the buck turned aggressive. Once I calmed back down, though, I realized the show was almost over. The buck was on his last legs, and I knew he would allow me to approach closely again. Hopefully, this next encounter would occur in more open terrain.

I slowly moved forward, searching for the buck with each step. This time, I reduced the far limit of my visual field to twenty-five yards. I didn't want any more dangerously close meetings. I hadn't gone forty yards when I noticed the buck lying twenty yards below me. He was on the side hill above the brook, substantially concealed by brush and the curvature of the land. I very carefully maneuvered to within fifteen yards. When I had a clear, can't-miss path to the buck's neck, I sent my final slug on its way. To my great relief, it connected solidly and the buck's upright head dropped to the ground. After a few final breaths, the buck was dead and my ordeal was over!

Understandably, I was tired, both mentally and physically. However, my day wasn't yet done. In fact, I already understood that the work that remained couldn't be accomplished in a single day. I only had thirty minutes of daylight left, and I was a long way from nowhere. The best I could do at this point in the afternoon was field-dress the buck and get myself safely out of the woods. Retrieving the deer would just have to wait until the following morning. I didn't like the prospect one bit, but that was the realty I faced.

The circumstances even robbed me of my chance to savor the moment. Here I was with my very first antlered buck, and all I could contemplate was the work ahead. Any celebration would have to wait until much later. I took a hurried glimpse at the buck's antlers, and commenced my knife work in the rapidly fading light.

As I had expected, my initial shot had struck the deer a little far back, hitting the guts. There was no exit hole. Once finished, I positioned the buck so that he would drain well, threw the heart and liver in a plastic bag, and headed back towards the road.

I had no idea whether anyone else in the original group was anywhere near. Despite the fact that I hadn't seen a soul in six hours, I really didn't think the other guys would abandon me, though. And if they were in the neighborhood, they had undoubtedly heard the shooting and anticipated that something was up.

I was relieved to finally see Richard Estes well before I reached the road we had originally used to access these woods. The bag of organ meats I carried provided evidence that I had experienced success, and I related my tale as the two of us walked back to the vehicle, which we reached in the dark. I told him and everyone else I spoke to that night that I had killed a $2^1/_2$-year-old eight-pointer that weighed between 130 and 140 pounds.

Richard graciously offered to help me get the buck out of the woods early the next morning. I arrived home well after dark, where I was able to recount the day's events for my wife. Janet had begun to wonder if something had happened to me. I also called my father to share the news. I was completely exhausted by this time. I had been walking almost non-stop for the entire day, plus the emotional toll had been enormous. And still, the worrying wasn't over. Until I had physical possession of the buck, I wouldn't be able to relax.

Not unexpectedly, I didn't sleep well that night. I couldn't help but consider all the potential negative consequences of leaving the deer overnight. My mind kept conjuring the possibilities, with emphasis on the negatives: Would it be difficult to find the deer? Would another hunter discover the buck before I could get there? Would animals eat my trophy? Would the meat be spoiled? How hard would it be to drag the buck to a road? Today, with the advantage of vastly more experience, I would shrug many of these concerns off. Back then, however, dismissing such thoughts was quite impossible for a twenty-eight-year-old who had just killed his second deer.

I met Richard and Kenneth at the Estes family store early the next morning. It had snowed a bit overnight, but not enough to impact our search for the buck. I explained as best I could where the deer was located. After discussing the matter, we decided the easiest route out of the woods was to drag the buck to a road beyond where I had been the day before. Richard and I would retrace my steps back to the deer, and Kenneth would periodically check the destination road by vehicle later in the morning.

With a seemingly sound plan in place, Richard and I started on our way. We had no trouble finding the buck, which had a light dusting of snow on his back. Fortunately, he hadn't been touched by any other critters. There were only two remaining issues to contend with. First, the drag was going to be uphill, and severely so to start. Second, much to my dismay, the buck had lost two points during his overnight stay.

Don't get me wrong; there was no damage to the buck's antlers. I had simply miscounted points the previous afternoon due to my excited state of mind and the time constraints which burdened me. The fact that the buck had been demoted to a six-pointer was of little actual consequence, except for the minor embarrassment it caused me.

Richard and I pulled on the deer in tandem to get us up the brook embankment. After a brief rest at the top, we continued towards the road, taking turns as we went. Just as we approached the way, we thought we heard the snow-muf-fled sound of a vehicle. It was Kenneth slowly chugging up the hill, looking for us as he drove. Talk about perfect timing. After hailing Ken, we threw the buck into the back, and we arrived at the store well before noon. I certainly appreciated all the assistance I had received.

It was only then that I was finally able to relax and enjoy my accomplishment. A subsequent trip to the checking station pegged the buck's weight at 136 pounds, right in line with my guesstimate. At that time, I was living in Pittsfield where I had no garage, so I hung the deer at my parents' house in Dalton.

The decision whether or not to have the buck mount-ed was a no-brainer. Given the few successes I had enjoyed during my first dozen or so years of hunting, I logically imagined that I might never again shoot a buck this good. Thankfully, the aforementioned sentiment regarding my future as a deer hunter couldn't have proved more wrong.

As I reflect on this hunt all these years later, a couple of things strike me. First, I wasn't a particularly skilled marksman, opting to throw plenty of lead around, rather than taking a single well-placed shot. This hunt helped me realize that I needed to not only improve my shooting abili-ties, but to be more patient regarding shot selection.

Second, on a more positive note, I may have been lucky to encounter the buck, but good fortune wasn't entire-ly responsible for killing and tagging him. I methodically sifted through an extensive and complicated array of sign, drew the correct conclusions from the evidence, and reacted accordingly. Sure, I made some minor mistakes. But, there's no doubt in my mind that the entirety of the experience was a very valuable learning tool, and that it helped me become a much better hunter from that moment forward. The fact that I had been forced to do all this on my own helped foster a strong sense of self-reliance, an essential attribute for a budding tracker.

Finally, when you haven't fired ten total shots at deer in as many years, you might reasonably conclude that ten rounds would be more than enough ammunition for a single day's outing. As I learned on this hunt, you just might be proven wrong.

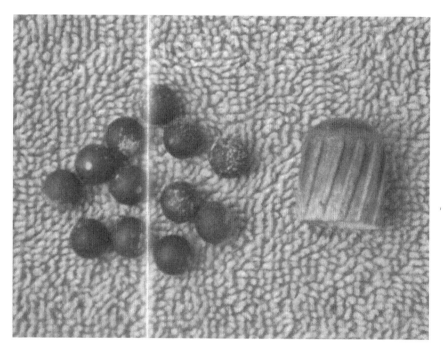

Sorry, I can't recommend buckshot (l) for hunting deer. Rifled shotgun barrels and saboted slugs are rapidly replacing traditional Forster-style slugs (r).

*My very first antlered buck, after more than a decade of hunting. At the time,
I honestly thought I might never kill another deer as good as this one.*
Photo by Charles Carter

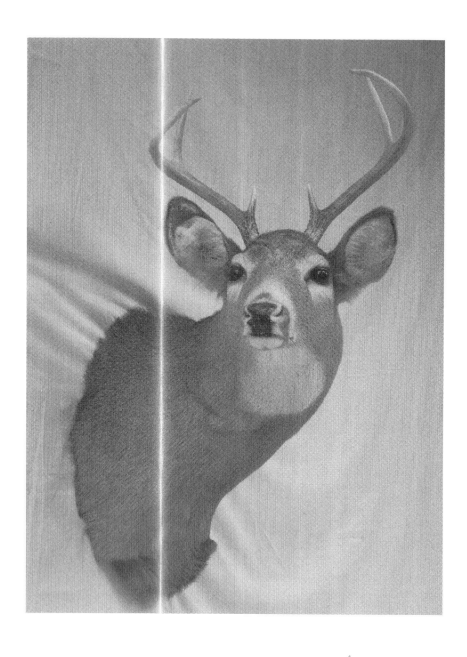

TRACKING AS A TEAM SPORT

Mention tracking whitetail deer and most people conjure a scene deep in the woods, a single hunter, alone and unconcerned, stealthily pursuing his or her quarry. Indeed, that vision is quite representative of the practice of tracking, at least in its purest form. Several of the preceding stories detail hunts that took place under such circumstances. In fact, most of the deer I've killed over the years were taken far removed from other humans, even if the hunt began with me being part of a larger group.

The sad reality is that days such as those mentioned in the previous paragraph are few and far between. Elsewhere in this book, I've offered my opinion that conditions conducive to killing a deer while tracking only exist on a handful of the available hunting days in any given season. On the vast majority of days the ground is bare, too little snow is present or the snow which does exist is excessively noisy. These circumstances have one thing in common: they make it nearly impossible to single out a deer and effectively sneak into shooting range.

So what's a tracker to do when the weather doesn't cooperate by providing good tracking snow? Well, staying home is an option, but it's hard to kill a deer from your couch. A more effective approach is to hunt with friends or family on such days. Teamwork can produce results when going it alone can't. Show me a little snow, a good tracker and at least one other hunter who knows the local deer and their habits, and I'll show you some dead deer on the meat pole by season's end.

The following stories illustrate two different occasions when conditions necessitated a change in tactics from hunting solo to a group effort. Nonetheless, in both cases, tracking was an essential component of the hunt. Indeed, if I hadn't been able to find the bucks and keep them moving, they would have never become targets for my partners.

The first hunt took place in December of 1991. A few inches of snow covered the ground, which was a plus. Unfortunately, the snow which was present wasn't the right type. A period of above-freezing temperatures had been followed by a sudden cold snap. As a result, the moist and melting snow which had been present was quickly transformed into something far less desirable.

This new formulation more closely resembled a loose conglomeration of frozen ice balls than individual snowflakes. Not surprisingly, with each step in the stuff a loud, distinctive "crunching" sound was produced. I had no doubt that a deer would be able to zero in on the resultant noise from at least 100 yards away. Before I even entered the woods, I knew that my prospects of eventually taking aim at any buck I might be fortunate to track was, for all intents and purposes, zero.

Like so many times before, my father, Al Cady and I headed to Windsor to hunt. We decided to concentrate on a fairly small parcel of land that we all knew intimately. Al and my father posted up while I went searching for deer. Although far from ideal, the snow still allowed me to distinguish between tracks made by bucks and does, an important advantage. And as expected, the icy consistency made for very noisy walking.

I cruised through the traditional deer hangouts looking for fresh tracks, one small section of woods at a time.

Around mid-morning, I jumped a couple of deer from their beds shortly after I intercepted the tracks. Of course, I never saw the deer when they bolted out in front of me. I'm sure they had been alerted to my approach long before I was within visual range. Plus, the deer knew I was dogging their tracks and not likely to merely pass through the area.

One track was medium in size and the other was smaller. As I looked over the spoor carefully, I grew confident that the sign had been made by two bucks, a yearling and an older deer. Both prints were larger than those found in the run-of-the-mill doe-with-fawn scenario. Plus, to my eye, both tracks displayed the distinctive heart-shaped configuration typical of bucks. Given that the rut had long since concluded, I wasn't at all surprised to find two bucks hanging out together.

Now that I had the ostensibly antlered deer on their feet, I intended to keep them moving in an attempt to run them by one of my hunting partners. If I had been hunting with the benefit of decent conditions, I would have elected to pursue these bucks differently. My pace would mirror that of the deer. I would move rapidly when the bucks were running, and I would slow to a creep when the sign indicated the animals were preparing to bed.

On this day, my odds of even seeing the bucks, let alone getting a shot, were exceedingly small. Although I remained alert to the possibility, I wanted the deer to be more concerned with what was behind them than what might lie to their front. Therefore, I trailed the duo at a steady but swift pace. In essence, I was giving myself up for the greater benefit of the group. This behavior was less about being unselfish or magnanimous, and more a conscious acknowledgement that, given the noisy conditions, this was the best way to kill a deer.

I ran the two believed-to-be bucks around for the rest of the morning. Not unexpectedly, I never heard nor laid eyes on them the entire time. Despite my efforts, the bucks managed to avoid running by either of my cohorts. Eventually, the animals crossed a dirt road and entered a new section of woods around noon. I left them there and went looking for my father and Al.

We took a break for lunch, another long-time staple of our hunts in Windsor. More often than not, I viewed these interludes as unnecessary interruptions which detracted from the task at hand. On this day, however, the pause was most welcome and perfectly timed. The bucks would settle down within their new surroundings once they realized I was no longer in hot pursuit.

For some long-forgotten reason, Al was unable to hunt in the afternoon. He headed home, which left just me and my father to "gang up" on the bucks. To be honest, I was so certain about what would happen next, having more than two people on hand seemed like overkill. Moreover, the whole affair could be expected to be over in roughly thirty minutes. With any luck, at least one buck would fall to my father's shotgun.

Let me explain the reasons for my optimism. The parcel the bucks had entered was fairly small. More important, I was aware of a heavily used crossing about a mile from where I had temporarily abandoned the tracks. The aforementioned deer run was situated at the top of a hill along a second dirt road which intersected the first one. Experience gained over decades informed me that this place was the odds-on favorite for where the bucks would head once I got them running again.

I gave my father explicit instructions regarding where and how to position himself, as well as details regarding the animals he could expect to see. After waiting an appropriate period of time, I took up the tracks once more. I hadn't traveled 300 yards when I heard the bucks scramble out of their beds well in front of me. I immediately increased my pace as I followed the running tracks.

The two deer started down the hill before gradually swinging to the south. That was the first confirmation that my plan might play out as I had expected. I knew it wouldn't take long for the fast-moving deer to navigate the remaining cover between me and my father—no more than ten minutes. With each step I took, the tension continued to build as I waited for the hoped-for blast of my father's shotgun.

I was still several hundred yards removed from his expected position when I finally received the report I had been anticipating. A single low-pitched boom echoed back to me from my father's general direction. Under the present circumstances, I had no expectations that either of the deer would reverse course and come my way, so I continued along the tracks.

When I at long last reached the road, I observed my father in the alders, bent at the waist and peering into the weeds. At first, I thought he might be attempting to follow a blood trail. A few seconds later, however, it became apparent that he had managed to knock over one of the bucks.

The deer, a fair-sized yearling with one busted antler, was dead when I arrived. After congratulating my dad, I listened to him recount the events of the past few minutes. He had been standing in a position where he could observe the deer run I had directed him towards. As the two bucks approached, they stopped momentarily in a place where my father could initially only see their legs. Once the lead deer advanced a couple of more steps, dad was able to confirm the deer was a buck. As soon as the buck's chest was exposed, my father took the opportunity to shoot. The deer ran a few yards to the west and went down.

Amid the chaos surrounding the immediate aftermath of the shotgun blast, the trailing deer reversed direction and disappeared. My father never saw what that buck wore on his head. Naturally, I was curious about the second deer's actions and whereabouts, so I followed his track. The buck simply traced a small button hook around my father and crossed the same road closer to the top of the hill.

This deer was definitely the bigger of the two, and I would have bet a sizable chunk of change that he possessed more antler than the buck my father had killed. Just for the record, in my experience, when two bucks are traveling together, the younger deer will be leading the older buck about seventy-five percent of the time. I've seen this behavior on multiple occasions.

After gutting the buck, we had a short, easy drag to the closest truck. Although plenty of time remained in the day we decided to call it quits, satisfied with our good fortune and grateful for our time together.

A week later, the two of us were hunting the same general area and I met another hunter. Instead of being secretive, the man was quite open as we discussed local hunting prospects, offering that he had repeatedly seen a single-horned yearling buck in the area during the bow season. Later in the day, I related this conversation to my father, adding, "I didn't have the heart to tell him the buck wouldn't be coming back."

++++++++

John Dupuis and I teamed up for a hunt during the muzzleloader season in 2008. Actually, my father was also a participant for the first half of the day. As in the previous hunt, the conditions weren't suitable for tracking, at least not the go-it-alone variety.

On this particular day, rather than an excess of noise, a lack of snow cover served as the primary impediment to singling out a buck for destruction. No more than an inch of

snow could be found anywhere. Many places contained less-
er amounts, and some areas featured bare ground. Generally,
the woods were about one-third brown and two-thirds
white. In shaded areas on north-facing slopes, for instance,
white covered most of the ground. Woods with southern
exposures, except for the occasional pocket, tended to be
brown with leaves.

The three of us entered the woods with rather low
expectations. We elected to hunt a section of woods that the
deer had been favoring during the earlier shotgun season.
John and my father took up stands in locations which covered traditional escape routes. For my part, rather than
actively searching for tracks, I planned to crisscross the area
in an attempt to move deer, hopeful that any animals I disturbed would eventually be seen by my compatriots. In the
course of my travels I would keep a watchful eye for any
deer tracks I might encounter, especially those belonging to
males of the species.

I spent the next couple of hours tramping through the
available cover. Deer and deer sign were both in short supply. Late in the morning I accidentally happened upon a
track I thought belonged to a buck. The spoor wasn't terribly fresh. Undoubtedly, it had been made hours before, closer to dawn. In addition, the day had since warmed, causing
further deterioration not only to the track's detail, but in
tracking conditions generally. As the day wore on, the bare
spots were growing in size as the snow melted and receded.

There was just enough snow that the deer could be
followed, albeit inefficiently so. I needed to search for practically each and every hoof print, which made for tedious
work. When the animal traversed a large area which happened to be snow-less, I would temporarily lose the track,
only to re-acquire it at the next available snow patch. I was
able to continually advance, but the process was time-con-
suming. Despite the difficulties, I was also lucky. If more

animals had been present, I would have found it that much harder—if not impossible—to isolate the buck's track, resulting in additional delays. And time is a valuable commodity when tracking deer.

For the solo tracker, the time-intensive nature of tracking in marginal snow conditions is a problem. However, the main reason for electing not to go it alone on such days is that a tracker spends an inordinate amount of time staring at the ground in an attempt to correctly read the sign. Naturally, it's impossible to search the woods for the deer in front of you while your attention is primarily directed downward. For these reasons, by this point in the day, I was pretty much resigned to the fact that I wouldn't be doing any shooting. Nevertheless, the opportunity still existed for me to be an effective hound and help someone else kill a deer.

Persistent effort, aided by attention to detail, allowed me to follow the buck to his chosen bedding site at the top of a steep drop-off. Of course, by the time I arrived, the buck was long gone. He had undoubtedly seen my plodding approach, even as my gaze continued to be fixated on the ground. I trailed the running deer a short distance, until I was able to determine the buck wasn't headed towards either of the waiting standers. I then left the track to gather John and my father and regroup.

Despite the fact that I had a viable prospect up and running, my dad decided to call it quits for the day. John, as always, was still game. We had the entire afternoon to hunt the buck, assuming I would continue to be able to ferret out the track.

I told John I was positive the deer was a buck, but the scarce information I had been dealing with hadn't allowed me to form any firm conclusions regarding the animal's size. So far, my effort was analogous to attempting to track a fire utilizing the smoke instead of the flames. I knew the deer wasn't a monster. My best guess was that I had found a year-ling or a two-and-a-half-year-old.

Based upon my description of where I had jumped the deer and where he headed immediately thereafter, John thought he knew a good spot from which to intercept the animal during the second leg of the hunt. I expected the buck to bed down shortly after he realized I was no longer in pursuit. John proposed to stake out a position well in advance of the deer's anticipated short-term movements.

Given the time it would take for John to reach this new location and the expected slowness of my subsequent tracking effort, we both figured this would be a one-shot type of deal. Our success would depend, in large part, on John's knowledge of the local deer and their habits, as well as my ability to tenaciously adhere to the buck's track and keep him moving.

I waited in place for about forty-five minutes, giving John ample time to make his move, and then started on the track. As the day warmed the tracking conditions continued to deteriorate. Fortunately for me, the buck was headed to the north and the shaded backside of a nearby hill. At this juncture, in order to stay on the track, I needed all the help I could get. If the deer had gone in almost any other direction, I would have most likely been unable to follow.

As things existed, tracking was possible but certainly not easy, especially over the next 400 yards. I methodically plodded along, careful not to be waylaid. I spent nearly the entire time with my eyes glued to the ground. After about an hour of painstaking progress, I heard what I thought was the sound of a running deer. The noise was so faint that I wasn't even able to discern the direction from which the clatter had emanated.

I was, however, pretty sure I had jumped the buck for a second time, and I received confirmation of that fact another 100 yards to my front. There I found the buck's vacant bed in the leaves, along with the running tracks of the fast-fleeing deer. My job immediately became a whole lot easier.

To this point in time, my progress had been painfully slow and snail-like. I was now able to advance by leaps and bounds, literally. With each jump the buck was leaving four deep imprints in the forest floor, churning up snow and leaf litter in the process. The resultant sign was much simpler to visualize and follow.

I didn't know exactly where John was positioned, but the buck chose to swing around the hill in his general direction, which was reason for some optimism. Encouraged by this turn of events, I resolved to keep the deer moving. I could only hope the buck's path brought him within shooting range of my friend.

I had progressed a few hundred yards beyond the buck's bed when I received the first indication that our plan might have succeeded. From several hundred yards ahead, the distinctive bellow of a muzzleloader broke the stillness. In my mind, that just had to be John doing the shooting.

It took me another five minutes to cover the ground that separated us. As I approached John's stand location I could see him bent over at the waist, presumably inspecting a dead deer. After a few more steps I could make out the deer's brown form amongst the mottled backdrop. Our combined efforts had paid off! Seconds later, I promptly congratulated John on his excellent shooting, not to mention his choice of stands.

I was understandably curious regarding the buck's size and what he wore on his head. I had put quite a bit of effort into this deer, despite the facts that I'd never even seen him and I really wasn't sure how big he was. The buck carried a smallish eight-point set of antlers. By all outward appearances, the deer looked like an average two-and-a-half-year-old, with an expected field-dressed weight between 130 and 140 pounds. I was pleased, since those incidentals were on the high side of my assumptions.

Next, John related his version of the hunt to me. He saw the buck loping through the hardwoods well before he pulled the trigger. The deer steadily approached from John's right. When the buck closed to within forty yards my friend grunted, bringing the deer to a sudden stop. With a standing, broadside target at relatively short range, it was a simple matter to place the bullet through both lungs, quickly ending the deer's life.

I assisted while John gutted his trophy. That job done, we contemplated the best way to remove the buck from the woods. The easiest route was downhill, but that direction would only serve to further separate us from our trucks. In the end, I offered to drag the deer to an accessible spot at the bottom of the hill, while John returned to his truck. Once he had reclaimed his vehicle, John would drive to our pre-determined meeting place and retrieve me and the deer. All things considered, our respective labors ended up being more or less equivalent.

These two separate hunts vividly demonstrate how teamwork can be used to produce successful outcomes when tracking conditions are less than optimal. In both cases, a gang of hunters wasn't required to see results. Instead, just two people, each with an important role to play, were needed to tag a deer. I could have easily provided many more such examples. Of course, not all team hunts end so favorably. Deer just aren't universally predictable. To be honest, the sport would be less appealing if success came too often or with too little effort.

Although I embrace and enjoy solitude in the woods, there's something to be said for the distinctly different pleasures derived from collaborating with others, the expenditure of mutual effort in pursuit of a common goal and the sharing of experiences, both good and bad. Whether teamed with friends or family members, human-to-human interaction shapes each of us, often in ways we don't anticipate or fully appreciate at the time.

The bonds so forged, in the woods or elsewhere, can be enduring and provide sustenance on difficult days. I retain specific details regarding each deer I've ever killed. I can just as easily summon the faces and words of my hunting companions—my father's look of approval for a job well done; a friend's gratitude for my assistance; and the gleam in my son's eye upon killing his first deer. None of these equally special memories would exist if I had elected to always hunt alone. I fully appreciate the fact that I'd be diminished by the absence of such experiences.

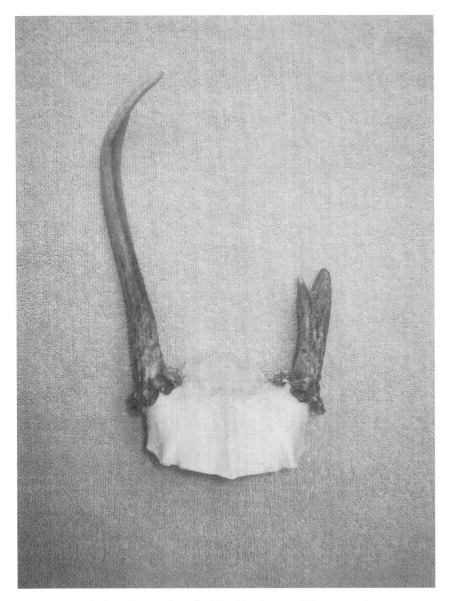

The buck my father shot, as described in this chapter. His companion most likely carried more bone on his head.

*Friend John Dupuis with two bucks taken during the 2008 hunting season.
The eight-pointer on the right is the one I tracked with the benefit of very
little snow.*

Photo Courtesy of John Dupuis

BUCKS IN BUNCHES

For those who hunt only during the rut, what I'm about to relate may seem completely foreign, something beyond your experience. The gun hunting seasons in my home state of Massachusetts occur in December. In most years, the annual mating season is either winding down or entirely over by then. The later in the month you go, the more apparent this reality becomes. Indeed, during the last two weeks of December, the bucks around here are often shedding their antlers. That activity doesn't take place until the does have been bred, supporting my previous contention.

As the breeding season comes to an end, something interesting happens. Bucks begin to reconstitute their pre-rut bachelor groups. I've personally witnessed this phenomenon so many times, I've lost count. Whereas many hunters envision bucks as solitary animals, I know differently. For most of the year bucks tend to hang out together. It's their "default setting," so to speak. Sure, there are exceptions where a particular animal, for unknowable reasons, chooses to live its life as a loner, but that's not the norm. Generally, it's only during the rut that bucks strike out on their own as they search for does.

I've already detailed one story where, not only were two mature bucks found together at this time of year, one of them was missing his horns at the time of my hunt. I could offer many more such examples. Yet, even in my neck of the woods, I'm frequently surprised to find other hunters who are either ignorant or dismissive of this concept. For instance, many will look at a small track in the company of a larger track and automatically assume the sign represents a doe with fawn. Sometimes that's accurate, sometimes not. It could just as easily be a yearling buck and a mature buck traveling together. A cursory look at the tracks won't provide the necessary information. Only a studied inspection, and the requisite know-how, will enable such a distinction to be made.

One time, in very difficult walking conditions, I followed three bucks much farther than I had intended. It was getting late, and I was about to turn back when I ran into another hunter. Since I was no longer interested in the deer, I offered this guy an opportunity to pick up where I was leaving off. Without fanfare, I told him the tracks all belonged to bucks. The gentleman promptly laughed and said, "Three bucks, huh?" I wasn't offended, but neither did I feel compelled to explain how I knew what I did. I just smiled, pivoted on my heels and left.

The hunt that follows occurred in mid-December of 2007, and it contains elements of the multi-buck phenomenon I referenced earlier. For some reason, I was completely on my own this particular day. More than likely, the weather was at least partially responsible for that. Although it had snowed overnight, by morning the precipitation had changed to a light freezing rain. This left a thin icy crust on top of the snow. With more drizzle forecast for the first half of the day, it looked like anyone brave enough to venture into the woods could expect a wet ass by day's end.

Nevertheless, I had a hunting spot in mind and I figured I would pretty much have the place to myself. I was optimistic I'd find deer, but killing one, not so much. I expected the top layer of ice would make walking rather noisy. When I exited my truck and began my hunt, my worst fears were realized. Each step produced a discernible sound, much like that produced when stepping on potato chips. The noise wasn't horrible, but it was certainly enough to seriously impede my ability to sneak up on deer. I quickly discovered that the heavier canopy found in stands of softwoods had protected those areas from the ice. Unlike the rest of the woods, walking in such places could be done quietly.

I first needed to find some deer, or at least some fresh tracks, so I began my serious search at the base of a nearby hill. Historically, deer had several places they used to go up and come down the hillside. The direction of travel varied based upon what interested the deer on any particular day. Sometimes, tracks could be found traveling in both directions. It was just those qualities which made this feature a logical starting point to my day.

I began at the northern limit of the mountain and proceeded to work my way south. I followed the hill's base just short of a mile without finding a single track. Apparently, the deer hadn't heard about my grand plan. Figuring the deer must be at a higher elevation, I then ascended the hill and began walking the crest in the opposite direction. This effort fared no better than had the first. Essentially, I had completed a large loop, returning to my starting point. Yet, I still hadn't found a single deer or any sign that might lead me to one.

Needless to say, I was disappointed and more than a little frustrated by this time. Nonetheless, I decided to give the area one last attempt before considering other options. Ultimately, I decided I needed to check out a place further south than I had ventured on my initial foray. This time, as a way of hedging my bets and covering even more ground, I cut away from the hill to the east and paralleled a small waterway southward.

Once again, deer sign was almost nonexistent. I was very near the point of quitting when I stumbled into the mother-lode of deer tracks. Suddenly, my prospects had gone from famine to feast. Apparently, the entire local herd of deer was concentrated in this tiny area, and I thought I knew why. From the sign available, it was apparent that the deer were feeding heavily on ferns, which this locale possessed in abundance.

To be sure, too many deer, along with too much sign, was preferable to the alternative I had been experiencing for most of the morning, but it still posed a problem. I had to sort all this out and hopefully come away with a buck worth hunting. Evaluating the spoor took some time, but I eventually reached some conclusions.

Although I hadn't seen a single animal, I had apparently scattered all the deer as I approached the area, as running tracks were everywhere. Of the roughly ten deer in the general area, I found where four different bucks had been feeding together. The largest of the bucks chose to vacate the area accompanied by most of the smaller deer. This group headed north. The remaining three bucks headed west, straight up the hill, together.

I now had two distinct choices available to me. I could hunt the biggest of the bucks, but that would entail tracking a rather large contingent of deer. Of course, it was possible that the buck might eventually peel away from the others, whereupon I'd have him to myself. But if the buck didn't separate from the larger herd, I could be in for a discouraging afternoon, bumping into satellite members of the group without ever seeing the buck. On the other hand, each deer in the second cluster could be expected to carry antlers, so my odds of seeing a deer I could actually shoot were much higher. Therefore, I opted to hunt the band of brothers.

I didn't relish another trip up the mountain, but I plodded along behind as best I could. The three bucks didn't stop running until they reached the top of the hill. As the bucks slowed to a walk, I was better able to decipher track detail in the moist snow. I was certain I had two yearling bucks in front of me, in addition to a single 2$^1/_2$-year-old. Once the terrain flattened out, the bucks wove their way through a series of hemlock swamps—essentially small depressions dominated by hemlock and spruce trees.

On the north edge of one of these topographical features, one of the smaller bucks suddenly veered to the south, while the other two continued west. For the time being, I decided to see what the loner was up to. I could always return to the other deer later, if circumstances warranted the change. Of course, I had no way of knowing for sure, but I suspected that this solitary buck had grown tired of running and was actively seeking a place to bed. Given the current weather conditions, the softwoods offered nearly ideal shelter from the elements.

The buck meandered along the western edge of the ten-acre swamp. I found myself making far more noise than I would have preferred as I followed behind. Plus, as each minute passed, I was becoming more convinced that I would find the buck bedded somewhere up ahead. I quickly made a tactical decision to leave the track and enter the swamp, where I could walk relatively quietly.

I rarely distance myself from a track I'm actively following, but this situation practically begged for such action. Although I couldn't be sure that the buck was even present, I also decided to proceed as if the deer was lying somewhere in front of me. That meant I would advance in stealth mode. If I didn't encounter the buck by the time I reached the southern end of the depression, I would get back on the track and re-evaluate the situation.

The effort very well might have proven to be a complete waste of time, but on this occasion my instincts were spot on. Step by step, I picked my way through the swamp, placing my feet on mossy hummocks whenever possible, while picking apart the brush with my eyes. Eventually, I approached the southern limit of the softwoods, where I could see into the more open hardwoods beyond. I suddenly heard some sticks snap to the left of me in the swamp. Unbeknownst to me at the time, the buck had circled into the softwoods from the south and had been bedded just inside the southern limit of the swamp. I don't know whether the buck had heard, seen or smelled my approach, but he was on his feet and running before I laid eyes on him.

The deer was headed out into the hardwoods at full speed. I didn't presently have, nor did I anticipate having, any kind of a reasonable shooting opportunity, at least not from my present location. Nonetheless, I hadn't given up hope just yet. As soon as I recognized nothing good was going to happen if I stayed put, I started running, as well. I advanced towards the hardwoods, covering twenty yards as quickly as possible. Once I had better visibility and could follow the buck's path of retreat, I yelled at the top of my lungs. Though he was 100 yards away, the buck came to a screeching halt.

That was exactly what I had hoped for. As the deer stood looking back in my direction, I quickly aimed and fired at the broadside buck. At the shotgun's report, he took two more jumps and promptly bedded down. To me, this behavior suggested my slug had most likely hit the deer in the guts. Now that the buck was down, I didn't have much of a target at which to aim, at least not from my present location. I didn't want to press the deer, but I didn't want to leave him there to suffer for an extended period of time, either. Rather than wait, I decided to try and sneak a little closer and see if I could get a finishing bullet into the animal.

I was able to shorten the distance another twenty yards or so, whereupon I anchored the buck with a second slug. Even so, a third round at arm's length was necessary to finally put the buck out of his misery. I hate it when things end like that. I'd much rather have the animal dead before I arrive on the scene. Despite good intentions and my best efforts, that hadn't happened in this instance, and for that I was sorry. That the buck hadn't suffered more than five minutes was of some consolation.

As I had predicted from the track, the buck was a yearling. He sported three points and I estimated his weight at 110 pounds. Unfortunately for me, I found myself in somewhat of a no-man's land. I was a long way from anywhere, especially my truck, which I reckoned was close to three miles distant.

After examining the alternatives for getting the buck out of the woods, I finally settled on a southwesterly route. That would still entail a drag of two miles, but it would be almost entirely downhill. Once I reached the nearest road, I could only hope that I would be able to impose on someone's generosity to make a phone call. With any luck, I would be able to secure a ride home from my wife. If not, I could look forward to a roughly seven-mile hike back to my truck.

With the excitement receding, I dug out my trail mix for a celebratory snack and some well-deserved nourishment. After gutting the deer, I cleaned myself up a little, checked to make sure I hadn't left anything behind and started pulling. My watch informed me that the hour was approaching noon. I wasn't lost, but I wasn't exactly sure where I would ultimately end up, either. The icy coating on all the trees was somewhat disorienting, but my main problem was that I didn't have intimate knowledge of the country before me.

I hadn't gone too far when I intercepted a logging road. I knew that if I continued to follow the trail downhill, I'd eventually reach civilization. At one point, the road leveled off for a stretch before forking. That forced me to choose which branch to take. I discontinued the drag temporarily and reconnoitered both possibilities before resuming my march lower. I finally popped into the open where I could see a road. I left the buck out of sight back in the woods and covered the remaining 200 yards to the pavement.

I was a little surprised regarding where I found myself, but a long-time family friend lived right across the street. I called home but Janet was out, so I tried my parents next. Fortunately, I was able to reach my mother. My father was expected back soon, and once he returned they would come fetch me. A half hour later I could see my father's familiar truck approaching. My ride having arrived, I returned to the woods for the buck, which we promptly threw into the bed of the vehicle. Upon reaching my truck, we transferred the deer before going our separate ways.

I must say: It's nice to have friends and family when you're in a jamb. Despite the hour, the town roads still weren't particularly navigable, as the day-long drizzle kept things icy. I was soaked, but I had my buck and I was safe. A day that had begun rather inauspiciously had ended with a flourish. I took a nice buck on a day when, due to the noisy conditions, the odds had been stacked against me.

The key to the whole hunt, though, was recognizing the sign for what it was: three bucks traveling together in the aftermath of the rut. Upon viewing the three tracks, an off-the-cuff, uninformed analysis might have concluded that the sign belonged to a doe and her twin fawns. However, a detail-specific examination, aided by an understanding of post-rut buck behavior, would have revealed a different story.

The first step in taking advantage of the bunch-of-bucks scenario is an open mind regarding the possibility. The next step—the hard one—is acquiring the skills to consistently be able to differentiate between doe tracks and those made by bucks. It's also helpful to be able to correlate the size of a buck's track to his weight.

Regrettably, these topics are outside the scope of this work. For those who are interested in additional information, I shamelessly recommend my book, *Tracking Whitetails: Answers to Your Questions.*

Book in hand or not, it's fair to say that reading alone won't make anyone an expert. The only way for that to happen is to spend time in the woods honing skills. If nothing else, the next time you encounter a pair (or threesome) of tracks while hunting in December, at least consider the possibility that those prints belong to deer carrying antlers.

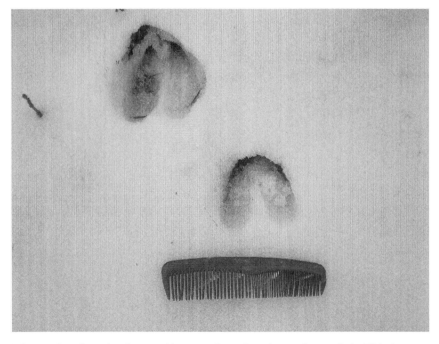

The tracks of two bucks traveling together after the rut has ended. This is a very common occurrence.

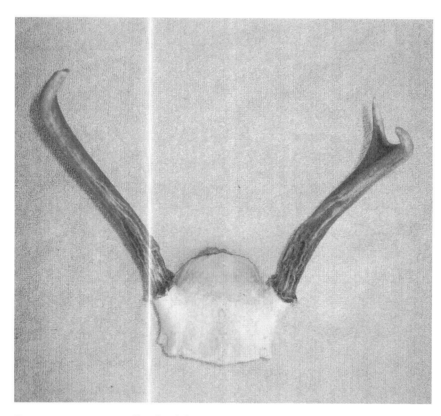

Just your average yearling buck horns. I have no way of knowing what the other two bucks this deer was initially traveling with wore on their heads, although one of them was undoubtedly a year older.

THE BIGGEST BUCK OF MY LIFE

In 1975 Larry Benoit wrote his classic volume, *How to Bag the Biggest Buck of Your Life*. For those readers who may not be aware, Larry is probably North America's most recognizable tracker of white-tailed deer. He once graced the cover of *Sports Afield*, where the headline read, "Larry Benoit—Is He the Best Deer Hunter in America?" Although Larry recently passed away, he and his sons who followed in his footsteps are widely considered to be royalty within the deer hunting community.

To be perfectly honest, Larry's book didn't contain much in the way of in-depth information regarding aging tracks in various snow conditions, differentiating between tracks made by bucks and does, and the like. As I related earlier in this work, for me, the book's primary influence was one of faith: the belief that what was possible for others, could be accomplished by me. Stated differently, I could succeed because others had succeeded first.

More than anything else, Larry's message allowed me to transform my hunting style to the one I was destined for— tracking. To be sure, all the pieces didn't immediately fall into place. Years passed before I was able to acquire the requisite skills. However, without the shove in the right direction offered by this single book, I doubt I would have made the transition to a full-fledged tracker. And without that transformation, I would have missed out on innumerable special experiences, all of which have greatly enriched my life.

The story detailing the biggest buck of my life dates to 1985. At that time, my dad, Al Cady and Billy Drew would typically journey to New Hampshire in early November. Once there, they would open up the trailer and ready everything for the deer hunting that would take place over the next ten days or so. While my three elders were present for the duration, I usually planned on stealing a couple of long weekends to join in the hunts. I'd leave home Thursday after dark and make it to camp by 9pm. When we were done hunting on the following Sunday, I'd return home. The routine would be the same the next week, except that we'd close up the trailer for the year and all of us would journey south together.

My first weekend in camp had passed without anyone killing a deer, which was pretty typical for our gang. There always seemed to be deer around, but lack of snow and the vastness of the woods tended to make for very low success rates. In fact, I had been hunting these mountains since the late 1960s and I still hadn't killed a deer! Nevertheless, we always had fun and every day was an adventure.

I arrived Thursday evening, hopeful that my second trip would be more productive than had the first. Before turning in for the night, I eagerly listened to the events that had transpired during my absence, hoping to glean some helpful insight into where we should hunt come morning. Tracking snow was still non-existent, and the weatherman offered no hope that any of the white stuff would be forthcoming, at least in those few days remaining to us. If something good was going to happen, it would necessarily have to be on bare ground.

The next day dawned cold and overcast. Rain was forecast for later in the day. Speaking of rain, this season had been one of the wettest in memory, as precipitation was an almost daily occurrence. So much rain had fallen over the previous two weeks that the lowlands were saturated and every brook and river was filled to capacity and roaring from the runoff. There was so much water that crossing such obstacles was no longer a routine event.

Bob Donnelly arrived just after sun up for breakfast. That put the day's hunting party at five members strong. Generation-wise, we had things pretty well covered. I, of course, was the youngest. My father and Al were contemporaries, children of the late 1920s. Bob and Billy were the oldest members of our group. They had been hunting these woods since Moses was a young pup.

Deciding where to hunt was always interesting. Nobody ever seemed to care where we went, at least until somebody else offered an opinion. Then, the other participants would either find fault with the pending suggestion or offer a "better" alternative. After a few minutes of good-natured give and take, some consensus would always be reached. For this particular morning, we elected to first push a small area north of camp, on the east side of the road where the trailer sat.

We referred to the spot as the "castle" because, years earlier, someone had built a small plywood fort for their kids in the middle of the woods. It didn't take long to thrash through the rather small triangle of timber. For my part, I didn't even see much in the way of fresh sign during my travels. I imagine my displeasure or impatience boiled over, because when I encountered my father at the end of the drive I said something to the effect, "There aren't any deer around here," in a decidedly disgusted tone.

My pessimism wasn't completely unbridled, though. The second half of the morning's game plan still awaited. The follow-on effort involved the parcel of land on the west side of the road. After waiting a sufficient period of time for the standers to redeploy, I began my stroll through the adjoining cover. For the most part, I was situated at the junction of two vastly different vegetative zones. The country to my left consisted of mixed woods on a side hill. I was near the bottom of the slope. A large swale-grass swamp dominated the landscape on my right. With all the recent rain, this area was pretty much flooded.

I was meandering back and forth along the lower third of the hill as I made my way west. Occasionally, I'd drift into the flats bordering the swale grass. About 200 yards into my effort, I heard the distinct sound of running deer in a small stand of alders about fifty yards to my front. I didn't see the animal or animals, but I was positive I had jumped at least one deer. I stood in place for a few minutes, and then all was quiet once again.

I decided to enter the alders and pick up the track, hopeful that I could keep the quarry moving in the direction of the standers. Before I had taken two steps, however, I heard something which changed my mind. The sound of water flowing through the center of the swamp had been a constant and continuous companion to this point. However, I suddenly realized that there was an added component to the watery rush. I heard what sounded like the distant sloshing of footsteps. To me, that could only mean one thing: the deer I had roused was likely crossing the swamp.

The patch of alders jutted out into the swale grass about twenty yards, preventing me from seeing up the lowlands. I quickly took a few steps to my right in order to improve my vantage point. What I saw next took my breath away. In the center of the swamp was the biggest set of antlers I had ever laid eyes on! The buck's head seemed to float above the tall grass which shielded his body from view. He was walking steadily towards the woods on the opposite side of the marsh.

I quickly evaluated the situation and determined that my only opportunity would come when the deer exited the grass on the far side of the swamp. A small incline containing short vegetation would let me visualize the entire animal for a couple of steps before the buck was once again swallowed by brush. Unfortunately, the distance was rather long, approximately 125 yards, and the shot would have to be taken off-hand. It was that or nothing.

Based upon my current skill level, I would rate the shooting opportunity I was about to face as difficult but possible. Still, I don't believe I could put the bullet in the lungs more than eight times out of ten attempts. At that time, however, the opportunity seemed much more imposing. Most of the shots I'd taken at game covered less than half that distance. I'd never fired a bullet in excess of 100 yards, at least not off-hand. Plus, in true Benoit style, my .30-06 Remington pump gun was equipped with the requisite peep sight, which wasn't exactly a precision long-range aiming instrument. I wasn't willing to let the buck escape without trying, however. I would just have to concentrate and perform to the best of my abilities.

My wait may have seemed like minutes, but only a handful of seconds passed between my first look at the buck and the moment I pulled the trigger. As the big deer emerged from the tall swale grass, I quickly fine-tuned my aim and fired. The stiff recoil disrupted my sight picture, causing me to momentarily lose sight of the buck.

Failing to see him, I initially thought the big deer had escaped into the waiting tree line, but that seemed implausible. On closer inspection, I could see the buck trying to pick his head up off the ground, his body obscured by grass. The bullet had dropped the deer in his tracks!

I stood my ground as I watched the buck's last few futile attempts to raise his head. Then, the deer breathed his last and ceased moving. Everything had happened so fast, the whole episode seemed too good to be true. I was certain the buck was dead. Nevertheless, I wasn't willing to take any chances. I started walking directly towards the deer, just in case I had misjudged the previous events. Besides, the whole swamp looked pretty much the same, and I didn't want to risk taking my eye off the buck for fear of losing him in the veritable sea of swale grass.

I advanced nearly twenty yards, keeping the buck's head in view the entire time. By then, the standing water in the flooded plain was deep enough that my boots no longer prevented the ingress of water. I could have cared less. Then, quite unexpectedly, I heard a flailing noise in the water to my left. I quickly turned to see a spike-horn buck jumping through the water a mere fifty yards away, headed towards the hill on my left.

Almost instinctively, I fired when the buck's four hooves simultaneously touched ground as he prepared for his next bound. At the rifle's report, the deer collapsed and practically disappeared from view amid the water and grass. For the next few seconds my head was seemingly on a swivel. I swung back to my right, checking to make sure the big buck was still lying still. Reassured that nothing was amiss on that front, I snapped my head back to the smaller deer, which was still kicking some.

Although it probably was unnecessary, I decided to put a finishing shot into the spike-horn. With the shooting all over, and after one last check on the big buck, I dragged the smaller deer out of the water to the base of the nearby hillside. With two bucks on the ground it was time to get some help. The three well-spaced shots had undoubtedly alerted the others that something good had happened.

My father wasn't too far away and he arrived within fifteen minutes. Bob Donnelly showed up a bit later. They were both pleased to see me with the small buck, which they assumed had been the sole object of my shooting spree. With my face beaming I said, "Wait until you see the other one." I explained what had transpired, and pointed towards the location of the big deer on the opposite side of the swamp. From our present vantage point, however, no part of that deer was visible. For the time being, they would have to trust that I hadn't fabricated the big-buck portion of the story.

After some discussion regarding the deployment of resources, I decided to leave my rifle and the spike-horn with my companions. My father and Bob would gut that deer and snake it out of the woods, while I attended to the bigger deer.

Getting across the wet wasteland to the far side of the marsh was my first challenge. By walking upstream 100 yards, I was eventually able to ford the expanse by utilizing an old beaver dam. Once on the opposite side, I then worked my way back to the big buck's location. Thankfully, I didn't have any trouble finding him.

At the moment when I had taken the first shot, I had no idea how big the buck was, nor was I able to count points. I simply knew that the animal was mature and he sported an impressive set of antlers. It was only when I finally stood next to the deer that I realized just how magnificent the buck really was. The antlers sported eight points in total and almost perfect symmetry. The tines were exceptionally long, with the longest exceeding ten inches. With five-inch bases and an eighteen-inch inside spread, the rack was even better than I could have imagined. The buck's body was enormous, a fitting complement to the deer's horns. I had never been near a buck of this size. As I stood there in awe, I dared to dream that he just might exceed the magical 200-pound field-dressed weight.

Although it had nothing to do with the buck's physical size or antler configuration, there was one additional feature concerning the deer which was hard to miss. The top of the buck's head was absolutely orange in color. The explanation was fairly simple: The buck had a distinct predilection for the nearby and plentiful alders, which he had been rubbing with abandon all fall. In fact, the bases of his antlers were packed with the shredded remnants of the orange-colored inner bark.

I positioned the deer with his head a little higher than his hips, in order to facilitate the field-dressing effort. Part way through the job, it occurred to me that Bob and my father hadn't yet seen the buck. I gave the two of them a yell and held the big deer's head as high as I could. As they stared in my direction, I could clearly hear Bob exclaim, "By Jesus," in his unmistakable New Hampshire accent.

Always curious about bullet placement and performance, I carefully checked the deer's wound. My bullet took the buck high in the lungs. A fragment had nicked the spinal column, resulting in the deer dropping instantaneously.

Once both deer were gutted, we engaged in some long-distance give-and-take regarding where I should drag the big buck. My inclination was to head back in the direction of the road, but my dad thought I should strike out to the west, where I would encounter a logging road. The distance was about the same, so I did as my father suggested.

By the time I started pulling it was about 11am. I knew I was in for a tough time when my first yank only moved the buck about a foot up the bank, whereupon he slid back six inches as I loosened my grip. Under normal circumstances, I would have tied a rope at the base of the antlers, made a half-hitch on the deer's nose, and pulled using a sturdy dead branch as a handle at the other end of the rope. This arrangement would have allowed me to face forward as I advanced.

That procedure just wasn't going to cut it this time. There wasn't any doubt that this deer would end up at the taxidermist, so I needed to be exceptionally careful about the buck's cape. So instead of the aforementioned procedure, I used the buck's horns to lift his head and neck off the ground as I pulled, backing my way forward a foot at a time. I rested occasionally, and I also left the deer to reconnoiter and clear the path ahead every hundred yards or so. Although I was working terribly hard, at the same time, I was also basking in the glory of a successful hunt for a very special animal.

This side of the swamp was heavily tracked up. Even on bare ground it was easy to see the over-sized hoof prints the big buck had deposited in the hours preceding our encounter. The bucks had likely spent the pre-dawn hours in this general location before crossing the swale to the area where I had jumped them. When I disturbed them from their resting spot in the alder patch, the bucks attempted to retrace their steps through the swamp.

Initially, I figured the drag would entail something in excess of a half mile before I reached the designated logging road. Hours had passed and still I persisted in my solitude. Finally, as I neared the skid trail around 3pm, Bob Donnelly arrived on the scene. He couldn't help me drag due to his age, but he was certainly welcome company. Plus, he had a pair of dry gloves I could use. Bob explained that the others would show up shortly. They had borrowed a small lawn tractor that had a cart in tow, into which we could throw the big buck.

About the time Bob and I arrived at the trail, the tractor could be heard chugging its way towards us. That was fine with me, as I was pretty much spent! I hadn't eaten a thing since breakfast, nor had I ingested any fluids. It was just starting to rain as the tractor pulled into view. More than a mile remained until we would be safely out of the woods, but the walk seemed fairly easy without the buck's dead weight slowing me down. For the rest of the journey, my effort was limited to keeping the big buck from slipping off the cart, a much easier task than the one which had consumed half the day. By the time the party reached the truck it was dark.

We decided to immediately drive into town to have both bucks checked and sealed. My father tagged the smaller buck. Despite my fatigue, this was a moment I had been anticipating all day long. I was immensely curious regarding the buck's weight. When the attendant put the big animal on the scales, the instrument read 200 pounds with the buck's head still resting on the ground. Once the entire animal was suspended in the air, the official field-dressed weight registered a whopping 217 pounds!

Frankly, I was stunned. I thought the deer might go 200 pounds, but I wasn't even sure he was that big. To be honest, if I had known he was that heavy when I finished gutting him, I doubt I would have even attempted to drag the buck all by myself over that half mile of bare ground. And just for the record, the spike-horn tipped the scales at a hefty 129 pounds.

Next, we drove the deer over to Bill Donnelly's house, where we hung them in his garage. There, the bucks would be protected from the elements and unwanted scavengers, a luxury we didn't have at the trailer. After some rehashing of the day's events, we headed up the mountain to our home away from home. I was completely exhausted by then. Adrenaline had kept me going for most of the day, but I had long since used up my reserve. I kept drinking in an attempt to replace the fluids I had expended during the arduous day, but the thought of eating solid food made me feel ill.

I didn't sleep very well that night. Between my mind replaying the hunt and my muscle aches, shut-eye was in short supply. The next morning, my hamstring muscles felt like someone had thumped them with a baseball bat, a byproduct of my newfound dragging style. Several days would pass before they once again returned to normal.

A couple days later, we closed up the trailer, picked up the bucks and started for home. Once there, I had the pleasure of telling and re-telling the details of the hunt, as well as showing off the bucks, in the days that followed.

In the hunt's aftermath, I had the opportunity to consider several aspects of the hunt in greater detail. First, I thought it highly unusual that a yearling buck would be accompanying a mature buck in the middle of the rut. As I've stated, in a post-rut environment that's not uncommon, but witnessing this phenomenon during the second week of November was surprising. I can offer no rationale for this occurrence, just my observation.

Second, whether the presence of the younger buck was expected or not, I was certainly shocked that he had let me walk, essentially, right up to him. I contemplated a plausible explanation for this behavior. Here's what I came up with: The spike-horn was following the big buck across the swamp when the big deer suddenly went down fifty yards in front of him. I'm sure this confused the younger deer, causing him to freeze in place. Obviously, the spike-horn heard me sloshing in the water, but maybe he thought another deer was responsible for the noise. By the time I appeared from behind the screen of alders, it was too late.

Finally, I had killed two bucks when the bag limit was one per hunter. Whether this constituted a violation of the state's game laws, I still don't know. That's because I was (and remain) uninformed regarding New Hampshire's policy on party hunting. Some states allow such practices while others don't. I do know this: I never went into the woods that day with the intent to kill two deer. Hell, given my experiences to that point in time, I would have never thought it possible to see two different bucks during the same day, never mind kill two in the space of two minutes!

As I stated previously, when I shot the second buck my reaction was almost entirely instinctive. I knew my father was nearby and that the spike-horn would be tagged and checked. Without that knowledge, I believe I would have restrained myself from shooting at the second deer.

Nevertheless, I'd be less than honest if I didn't acknowledge the possibility that I may have inadvertently violated a game law. That aside, I'm very comfortable with my actions. Given identical circumstances, I believe most hunters would have behaved similarly.

Besides the beautiful mount which graces my family room wall, there's one lasting carry-over from this hunt. On those occasions when I have become unduly negative or disgusted by the apparent lack of deer sign or sightings, my father has always been quick to remind me of those long-ago spoken words made just minutes before my encounter with the big buck—"There aren't any deer around here." I must admit, there hasn't been such an occasion when I didn't deserve the good-natured retort.

The biggest buck of my life may not have been taken in true Benoit style—alone, deep in the snowy woods, after miles of tracking—but the feat was memorable nonetheless. I've always felt privileged to have taken such a grand animal. In my opinion, every serious hunter deserves one such trophy. Yet, I'm mindful that not everyone is fortunate enough to experience what befell me on that November day in 1985, which only makes me appreciate the event more.

Larry Benoit's classic book: a bit short on instruction, but long on motivation.

A semi-desperate note Bob Donnelly scribbled and left on the kitchen table of the trailer. He was not only informing Al of our whereabouts, but soliciting as much assistance as possible for the daunting task of getting two bucks out of the woods.

This photo was taken once I arrived home from New Hampshire. The legs of the spike-horn can be seen to the right.

Photo by Janet Carter

The trailer in New Hampshire, our home away from home during our annual November hunt. Many a good memory was made here.

Photo Courtesy of Al Cady

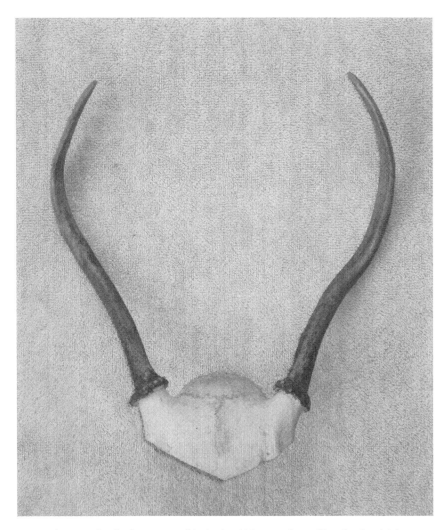

Not to be completely forgotten, this is the 129-pound yearling buck which was accompanying the huge eight-pointer.

ALMOST TRAMPLED

I'm often asked which particular skill is indispensable to consistently killing deer while tracking. To be sure, tracking is a hunting method which requires a rather large skill set. The physical demands are considerable, being able to accurately age tracks is important and discriminating between buck tracks and those made by does is crucial. The ability to shoot quickly and accurately at pieces of deer seen through holes in the brush is also essential.

However, someone can demonstrate expertise in all these areas and still fail to tag deer if he or she is incapable of seeing deer in the woods. Just for the record, I'm not referring to whole animals standing in plain view. Very few hunters would miss something so blatantly obvious. Nor am I speaking about running deer, their namesake white flag waving goodbye. If that's all you're seeing, you've likely already missed a bona fide opportunity to kill that animal.

Instead, I'm talking about recognizing small pieces of stationary deer, such as an ear or a portion of a leg. At other times, a deer's partial outline or an out-of-place color or texture might be the only clue that a deer is present. In the woods, when you're moving and the deer aren't, these are the very subtleties that must be appreciated in order to be successful. Unfortunately, this particular ability isn't one that can be effectively taught; it must be learned through experience.

Naturally, just like in other fields of human endeavor, wide variation in inherent skill exists from one person to the next. Whatever one's starting point, however, improvement is possible. Seeing deer is very much a success-breeds-success type of endeavor. That is, once you recognize a particular anatomical feature, silhouette or form for what it is, you're much more likely to identify the same visual clue when presented with it a subsequent time.

I've always felt that once I began to regularly see bedded deer, it heralded a quantum leap in my success as a tracker. Actually, if you know what to look for, deer which are lying in place often "stick out" more than well-concealed standing deer, at least in the presence of snowy backdrops. That aside, when you routinely encounter bedded deer you know you're doing two things well: picking up on the appropriate small visual distinctions and traveling efficiently and quietly through the woods.

I preface this story with these remarks because the following hunt dates to the period in my life when my tracking abilities were undergoing substantial improvement and, not coincidentally, a bedded buck plays a key role in the tale.

If my memory is correct, this hunt occurred on the first Saturday of the shotgun season in 1991. My father, Al Cady and I planned to hunt in Windsor that morning. Plenty of snow covered the ground. Even the evergreen boughs were heavily laden with the white powder, making the landscape picturesque. In the mixed-woods environment of our favored hunting grounds, this snowy backdrop made for quiet walking and reduced visibility. In most places, fifty yards was the farthest one could see in the woods.

The three of us started the day in a small section of forest near the top of Windsor Hill. We quickly encountered some tracks, but none of them were exceptionally fresh. According to my yardstick, only one of these sets of prints belonged to a buck. I was just as sure the deer wasn't exceptionally big—no more than 140 pounds and most likely smaller. After thrashing the immediate area for about an hour without stumbling upon any other hot prospects, I decided to track the lone buck we had turned up.

I estimated I was hours behind the buck, which I assumed had deposited this spoor well before daylight. Nonetheless, the sign was fresh enough that I was confident I'd find the deer in relatively short order, perhaps an hour or two. Almost immediately, the tracks crossed a busy highway and headed into the adjoining block of woods.

Once he was safely ensconced in this new parcel of land, the buck began a multi-mile excursion. By all appearances, the active rut seemed to have concluded, but this deer had many places he wanted to visit, nonetheless. The buck wasn't making scrapes or rubs, just checking his territory. In a few spots the deer stopped to feed, but not heavily so. I dutifully followed behind as the buck crisscrossed, doubled back and seemingly inspected every square inch of this rather large piece of country.

Despite my extensive travels, I wasn't seeing a lot of other fresh deer sign. I certainly didn't encounter any tracks made by a bigger buck. If I had, I probably would have switched to the larger track. There's something about a heavy buck that really stirs my soul. Though I always search such animals out, there just aren't that many of them available to hunt. And on any given day, there's no guarantee that I'll be fortunate enough to cross paths with a top-end animal.

For me, tracking is about hunting and the challenge it offers. All things being equal, I'll track the biggest buck available. However, I'm a pragmatist and not a purist. I'd rather be actively matching wits with any male of the species, rather than engaging in a day-long scouting session just because I couldn't find the biggest of tracks on a particular day. Therefore, I'll hunt what's available at the moment, even if it means the day's objective is a smaller buck. To do otherwise could entail enduring years, if not decades, between buck harvests, at least in my neck of the woods.

As I followed the wandering buck, I didn't sense that the sign was getting fresher. At least in part, that was because the buck wasn't spending a great deal of time in any one location. If the deer had stopped to feed heavily, for instance, I might have noticed the sign freshen considerably. I suspected that the entirety of the spoor I had been a witness to had been deposited before sunrise. Whether the tracks appeared incrementally less stale or not, I knew they would eventually take me to my quarry, and that's all that really mattered.

For all this time, the buck hadn't yet shown any indications that he was interested in bedding for the day. As the morning dragged on, I had to force myself to remain patient and vigilant. As miles of the status quo accumulated, I consciously resisted the sense of complacency that kept trying to creep into my psyche. I knew that the situation could change at any minute.

Intermittent snow squalls were becoming more prevalent as the morning slipped away. These bursts only served to reduce visibility further. After a couple of hours on the track, the buck's pace slowed as he skirted the edge of a swampy area. It was there that I saw something that quickened my pulse. I noticed that the buck had nibbled a few mouthfuls of browse as he passed by.

I immediately halted my progress and took a good look around me. To me, this sign was clear evidence that the buck was bedded nearby. My initial search revealed no trace of the deer. As I stood in place another snow squall enveloped the area, impeding my ability to explore the brush. With all my heart, I knew the buck was within 100 yards, but I was just as certain that, due to the driven snow and/or the gusty breezes, I was never going to see him! One way or the other, the deer would detect me and slip away, sight unseen.

Nevertheless, I resolved to do my best and let the chips fall where they may. I took a step forward, stopped and examined everything within visual range for sign of the buck's presence. When nothing of note was observed, I advanced along the trail another yard, careful to avoid making a sound. Once again, I came to a halt and surveyed every piece of the landscape. At the completion of my fourth such step, as I scanned the terrain on my left, the buck's head suddenly materialized through the snow flakes. The deer was lying in a depression at the base of a large hemlock tree, his attention fixed directly on me.

The range was no more than twenty yards! Instinctively, my shotgun snapped to my shoulder. With no change in the buck's posture, I had a choice to make. The deer's body was completely unavailable to me due to its position in the small bowl. Even the buck's neck couldn't be seen. I could shoot the buck in the head or not at all. As I peered down the barrel, the front fluorescent bead holding steady on the deer's nose, I really didn't see how my slug could miss its intended mark.

When I pulled the trigger, the buck's head snapped backwards as if he had been clobbered by a sledge hammer. I immediately advanced a couple of steps, gun at the ready. As I did so, almost unbelievably, the deer gave every indication that he was about to get to his feet. While the buck was still prostrate on the ground, I managed to aim and fire a second slug in the direction of the deer's chest.

From the moment I isolated the buck's head amid the swirling snow and softwood boughs until I executed my second shot, perhaps thirty seconds had elapsed. Though brief, the period had been filled with non-stop adrenaline. Although I had no way of knowing it at the time, the next half-minute would rival its predecessor for excitement.

Though grievously wounded, the buck still somehow managed to gain his footing. The deer was initially positioned facing away from me. Once ambulatory, the buck took a jump or two in that direction before quickly turning to the left. When he came broadside, I fired twice more in rapid succession at the running buck. As the echo of the fourth blast reverberated through the woods, the deer veered left once again.

In essence, the buck was tracing a small semi-circle around me. The deer wasn't moving as fast as an uninjured animal, but he was running. It's important to note that my interaction with the wounded buck was occurring in very close quarters. He was never more than fifteen yards distant and, in the aftermath of his most recent change in direction, the deer was now headed directly my way.

I had one more shell at my disposal, but the buck was just a handful of yards from my position and coming fast. I only had a split second available to me to decide what to do. I figured my health and welfare were higher priorities than putting yet another hole in the deer. Therefore, rather than shooting, I elected to dive to my right in an attempt to avoid being trampled or gored.

I made my lunge just in time. As I fell face first into the snow and rolled to my side, the buck motored by me on my left, within touching distance. Had I stood my ground, the deer would have most certainly run me over! I quickly spun around in time to see the deer take two more jumps before collapsing on the top of a brush pile. I had barely gotten back to my feet when the deer took his last breath and expired. The fifth round remained, unused, in the shotgun's chamber.

Talk about fast-and-furious action! I could scarcely believe what had just transpired. Two minutes earlier, I had all but given up on my prospects of even seeing the buck I had been tracking all morning. As things turned out, not only had I laid eyes on the deer, I had managed to kill him— but not before the buck nearly put the smack-down on me.

I required a few minutes to collect myself and calm down before I was ready to examine my trophy in greater detail. Understandably, I was curious about my shooting and the damage the slugs had done. I dragged the buck off the brush pile to garner a better look. My first shot had hit the buck square in the nose, causing tremendous facial skeletal damage along with profuse bleeding. Yet, no portion of the heavy lead projectile had reached the brain. The second slug had raked the buck's body from back to front. The heart had been hit, as well as the paunch. Of my final two rounds, one missed while the other had fractured a hind leg.

Either of the first two bullets would have proven fatal. I truly believe the buck would have bled to death in fairly short order as a result of the damage incurred from the first projectile. In the worst-case scenario, a follow-up shot may have been necessary had the buck managed to initially get away. Believe me; he wasn't going far. It continues to amaze me that a deer which incurred multiple fatal injuries while on the ground was still able to get to its feet and run that distance. Let no one doubt the whitetail deer's will to live.

With my curiosity regarding bullet placement and performance placated, I turned my attention to the buck's attributes. To me, he appeared to be a smallish two-and-a-half-year-old. The buck possessed an unremarkable but decent set of antlers sporting six points in total. In sum, the deer was about what I had expected from the time I first encountered his track.

The time was fast approaching noon. That wasn't a concern, but I had other worries. Specifically, I wasn't exactly sure where I was situated and, therefore, I was uncertain as to which direction I should drag the deer. I had no intention of retracing my many steps from earlier in the day. Through a process of elimination, south and east were my best bets. Roads were available in both directions. In the end, I decided on a southerly tack.

After gutting the buck and cleaning up, I started pulling. The going wasn't great due to the thickness of the vegetation, but at least the terrain was flat. After about 500 yards of concerted effort, I could see an opening in the woods to my front. I left the buck and went to investigate. As expected, the clearing signaled my arrival at a house lot along the road I had been steadily working towards.

I left the buck back in the woods and began the long walk towards my truck, electing to use the snow-less and obstacle-free road system instead of a more direct route through the forest. About half way to my ultimate destination, I received a pleasant surprise. My father and Al, who had been searching for me by vehicle, drove up and offered me a ride. They were happy to learn of my success, whereupon I interrupted to say, "Wait until you hear the whole story."

The three of us returned for the buck, which I quickly retrieved from its hiding place. Now that I had a better appreciation of the countryside, I realized I could have saved myself some effort by heading more easterly with the deer. Oh well. Although it was only 1:30pm, all three of us were done hunting for the day. We brought the buck to the checking station, where his official weight was recorded at 122 pounds.

In the hunt's wake, I had a chance to thoroughly evaluate the day's exciting events. While some might believe the buck consciously came at his protagonist with ill intent, I categorically reject that possibility. I've always believed the deer was simply dead on his feet and running blindly. His hop-scotch course, further affected by a broken rear leg, just happened to bring the buck to me in his last few desperate bounds.

Although I hope it never happens, I know that if someone smashed me in the face with a tire iron, I would find it impossible to make a considered decision regarding anything for a very long time. A subsequent bullet to the heart would only serve to magnify feelings of panic and spur instinctive, not reasoned, responses. Physiologically, I believe it's possible that the shock of my first bullet could have affected, even if only temporarily, the buck's ability to see, despite the fact that the buck's eyes seemed normal in appearance.

This was the very first buck I shot while lying in his bed. He wouldn't be the last. As a tracker, I consider such a feat to be the ultimate objective for my preferred style of hunting. This perfect result doesn't happen very often, but it's tremendously rewarding when it does. Still, although skill plays a significant role, I'd be lying if I claimed ability alone was responsible for a successful outcome. Luck, both good and bad, is a hunter's constant companion. An errant breeze at an inopportune time could have cost me this deer. However, on this particular day everything happened to work out perfectly. As a result, I emerged victorious in an uncomfortably close encounter with a buck—a situation that I certainly don't expect to experience a second time.

This is the Poly-Choke on the muzzle of the shotgun I used to kill the deer in the story. I superimposed the large fluorescent aiming bead on the buck's nose. I killed quite a few deer with this relatively simple aiming system.

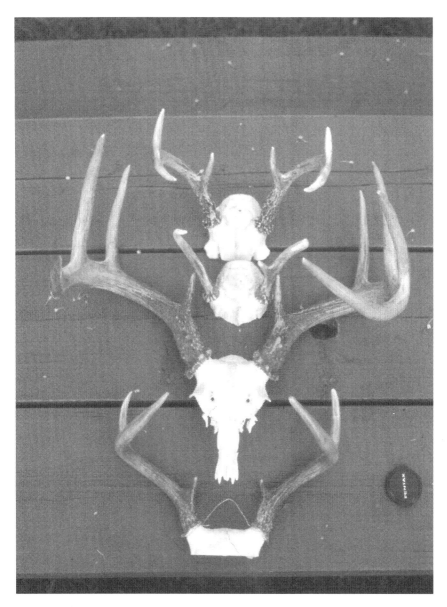

The 1991 hunting season was one of our more successful years, as this photo proves. Al Cady shot the buck at the top and my father killed the next one down. The bottom two belong to me.

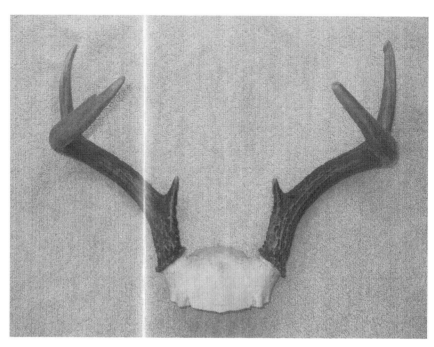

The first deer I ever shot lying in its bed. This buck weighed 124 pounds.

GOOD HUNTS COME IN SMALL PACKAGES

The shotgun season in Massachusetts, just like its counterparts in other jurisdictions, is a big deal. Years ago, this much-anticipated hunting window occurred during the first full week of December, Monday through Saturday. More recently, the season commences on the Monday following Thanksgiving and lasts two weeks, Sundays excluded. The 2005 shotgun season would prove to be one of the better years in my deer hunting experience. Earlier in this book I detailed a hunt in which I was able to kill a top-end buck on the final day. However, the season got off to an auspicious start with the following hunt.

My father, friend George Bigelow and I made plans to hunt Windsor for the day. We even had the benefit of a couple of fresh inches of snow on the ground. Unfortunately, the small storm had arrived shortly before dawn and the wet snow didn't stop coming down until nearly 8am. Of course, this poorly timed event had the effect of obliterating any tracks the local deer herd made as they foraged about just prior to bedding for the day. As a result, I had every expectation that the woods would appear to be completely devoid of deer when I began my hunt.

If the snow had ceased earlier, I might have been able to find a suitable track in any number of places. However, in a situation such as this, it's a fool's errand to roam the country blindly in search of fresh tracks. Sure, it's possible to get lucky and stumble across a set of prints made by a late-moving buck, but the odds aren't good. A better strategy is to concentrate on known bedding areas. Of course, that requires fairly intimate knowledge of the local terrain, as well as the habits of the animals which reside there.

Given the tract of land we decided to hunt, I was especially interested in a couple of stands of softwoods as potential bedding grounds containing deer. These areas, besides offering cover, contained small hills which provided good vantage points for the local deer, as well as shelter from the wind. Perhaps of greater significance was the fact that I had jumped animals from these places on previous hunts over the years.

My father and George took up positions in spots that offered decent chances of intercepting any deer I happened to get up and running. Meanwhile, I entered the woods from the opposite side of the rather large parcel and began my search. As I had expected, deer tracks were nonexistent. Fortunately, I didn't have to travel far before I discovered something positive—two oval-shaped bare spots in the snow beneath a hemlock tree.

The now-vacant beds belonged to a doe and her fawn. I hadn't seen them as they fled, but it was clear that I had been responsible for disturbing the duo's tranquility. Once I was able to surmise that neither deer wore horns, I continued on, hopeful that I'd enjoy a similar encounter with an antlered buck. Shortly thereafter, I discovered a third empty bed, some fifty yards beyond the first pair.

At first take, this finding looked promising. If this deer had truly been a member of the larger doe group, I would have expected the bed to be within spitting distance of the first two. It's not uncommon for bucks to bed in the general vicinity of doe groups. When they do, however, bucks normally distance themselves from the females and fawns. This scenario fit that description to a tee. Still, these observations were merely circumstantial evidence that I had come across a buck. The final determination would have to be made from the animal's hoof print.

Arguably, the most difficult task in tracking is to distinguish between the track of a mature doe and that of a yearling buck. Since both specimens commonly weigh 100-120 pounds (field-dressed weights in my hunting areas), differences in track size are minor, making this parameter an unreliable indicator of gender. Track shape is the key to being able to make this important distinction. Secondarily, behavior and/or urine patterns can also be helpful in making a determination.

Bucks, even those $1^{1}/_{2}$ years old, sport hooves that are wider at the rear than those belonging to does. This phenomenon tends to give the track left by a buck, yearlings included, a configuration which can be described as heart-shaped, not in the true anatomic sense but in the more-recognized Valentine's Day version. By comparison, the track of the female of the species appears more slender and delicate in appearance.

As a buck matures, his hooves continue to widen while the front of the toes round from wear, making this heart-shaped trait quite apparent. For a yearling buck, however, this identifying feature of track shape is less obvious and easily missed, especially when snow conditions are less-than-ideal. Even so, recognizing the track of the "teenage" buck is a task that can—and must—be accomplished, especially if you don't want to spend an entire day hunting an animal which is antlerless.

After thoroughly evaluating the tracks deposited in the vicinity of the third bed, I concluded the spoor belonged to a yearling buck. As was the case with the doe and fawn, this deer had departed in advance of my arrival and without my having seen him. I was just thrilled that my semi-

informed wanderings had been so quickly rewarded with a
hot prospect. I could now adapt from searching mode to full-
on hunting mode.

The deer I had singled out initially ran towards the
north, roughly following a small stream as he traveled. Once
he put some ground between us, though, the buck settled
down in short order. It wasn't long before the deer slowed to
a walk. By this time, it had begun to snow lightly, making
the tracks appear older than they actually were. I wasn't in
any danger of losing the trail unless the snow started accu-
mulating at a much higher rate, and that wasn't likely.

Shortly after the buck's pace slackened, near the con-
fluence of two small waterways, he turned east and headed
uphill along the south bank of one of the tributaries. I
slowed down considerably, in anticipation that the deer was
most likely bedded somewhere up ahead. I also expected
George to be posted where the stream I was paralleling exited a small pond, approximately a half mile further up the
hill. It was increasingly likely that one of us would eventually get a good look at the buck.

I continued to creep along, thoroughly scanning the
woods for sign of the deer at each step. Half way up the hill,
without warning or apparent cause, the track veered deci-
sively to my left. A sudden alteration in a deer's direction of
travel, especially when you have reason to believe the animal
is about to bed, is an important clue—one that just can't be
missed or mistaken.

In this case, the buck had chosen to make his turn just
beyond a large yellow birch tree. I had been able to notice the
deer's change in direction from five feet further back, whereupon I immediately froze in place. As a result, the birch tree
effectively screened my presence from the buck, which I
quickly identified some seventy yards away, bedded and
relaxed. Had I taken one more step forward, though, I would
have popped out into plain view of my prey. In all likeli-

hood, such carelessness would have resulted in the forfeiture of a golden opportunity.

As I had expected, based upon his modest antlers, the buck looked to be a yearling. Since I knew the deer's whereabouts and he remained oblivious to mine, I had the advantage. A quick check of the wind revealed that my scent wouldn't reach the buck, at least for the time being. Still, problems remained. Geographically, the buck was positioned a little higher than me, further reducing his already small profile and leaving me with very little viable target at which to shoot.

Using the birch for cover, I tip-toed the few steps to the base of the tree and carefully poked my gun from both sides in an attempt to find a decent line of fire to the buck's vitals. Although I was sorely tempted, I was forced to conclude that neither avenue offered a reliable chance to kill the deer. Sneaking closer wasn't possible, either. I carefully considered the other options available to me, such as trying to grunt the buck to his feet. Ultimately, I rejected these alternatives and decided to wait and see how things played out.

It wasn't particularly cold, so I knew I could last at least an hour before I'd be forced into choosing a different course of action. About fifteen minutes into my vigil the wind started to become less predictable, its direction edging ever so slightly towards a bearing which would bring my scent to the buck. Should the breeze swing directly to my rear, I knew the existing calm would be shattered in a flash, leaving me with, at best, a split-second opportunity to kill the deer.

Anticipating this eventuality, I readied myself by firming up my stance and bringing my shotgun to bear, index finger on the safety and supported by the birch. Seconds later, I felt cold air sweep along the back of my neck. Almost simultaneously, the buck rose to his feet and stared down the hill in my direction.

In a brief second, I managed to swing the red aiming dot of the EOTech sight into the buck's vitals and pull the trigger, dropping the deer back into his bed. I quickly pumped another slug into the chamber and hurried up the rise. My first shot, though fatal, had struck a little higher than I wanted. With the buck still flailing, I carefully placed a finishing round into the deer.

Just that quickly, the hunt was over! It was barely 11am. The buck looked to be a smallish yearling, weighing no more than 110 pounds. Instead of displaying single spikes on each side, the deer's antlers forked, making him a four-pointer. With the buck dead, I went looking for George, who had undoubtedly heard my shooting. I found him where I expected he'd be, some 300 yards higher up the hill.

We returned to the dead deer, whereupon I recounted the hunt's details to George before attending to the removal of the buck's innards. That task accomplished, the two of us discussed the particulars for getting the deer out of the woods. I finally decided the easiest route involved retracing my steps down the hill to where the brooks joined, and then swinging northward to the bordering highway. George would leave the woods the way he had entered and gather up my father. The two of them would then meet me at a pre-determined location on the road.

With any luck, my drag wouldn't involve too much arduous uphill work. Still, the projected course encompassed nearly a mile. Everything went pretty much as I had expected, and I arrived at the pick-up point about 12:30pm. To my great relief, my father and George pulled up at almost the same moment. I had worked up a pretty good sweat and I didn't relish the prospect of standing motionless for any length of time, exposed to the increasingly blustery wind. We threw the buck into the truck, and then stopped for some lunch before calling it a day.

Many readers may be wondering why I spend so much time describing my efforts to get dead deer out of the woods. I know that others consider a difficult drag to be an imposition and a distraction from the larger objective of killing a buck. To them, this time spent huffing and puffing in exertion is best forgotten, and the sooner the better.

While I don't pretend that skidding deer through the woods doesn't involve real effort, obviously, my viewpoint is quite different. Perhaps my outlook is shaped by the way I choose to hunt, where physicality is an essential, entrenched component of tracking deer. To me, this final phase of the hunt is just as meaningful and important as all those aspects which preceded it.

Searching for tracks, trailing deer, putting myself in shooting position, executing the shot and blood trailing, as well as retrieval and removal, all contribute to the overall experience. Consequently, I could no more claim I told the entire story while ignoring that portion of the hunt devoted to moving a buck out of the woods, than I could saw off my right leg and maintain that I was physically whole.

There's one additional consideration worth sharing. For me, having just taken an animal's life, the walk from the forest gives me time to relive those recent events, decompress and savor the moment. At no other time in my life am I better able to appreciate my role as a hunter in the larger circle of life and death. It's a time of reflection and tranquility.

All in all, this hunt exemplified deer hunting efficiency: find a buck; track a buck; kill a buck. Rarely do things fall into place so nicely, especially when the day begins with a total absence of deer tracks! Although I enjoyed my share of good fortune, skill played an important role in my success, as well. Being able to identify the track of a yearling buck and subsequently recognizing the signs of imminent bedding were crucial.

Would I have preferred to find a huge, magnificently antlered buck at the end of the trail? Sure. Would that have made the hunt any more exciting or satisfying? Not appreciably. For me, the thrill of tracking deer is in the chase: reading sign correctly, anticipating my quarry's next move, and my own decision-making and execution. Inches of antler and pounds of flesh have little bearing on the magnitude of the challenge, which is and always will be grand.

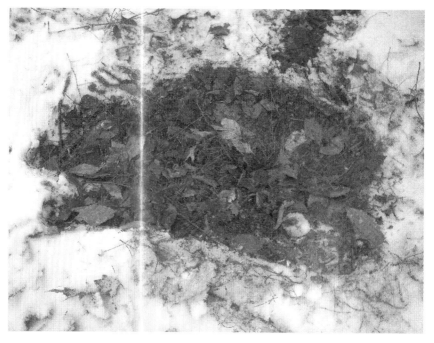

A brown melted oval in the snow, created by a bedded deer's warmth.

This is a yearling buck's track on bare ground. Compared to that of a mature doe, the track is wider at the rear, giving it a heart-shaped appearance.

This is the EOTech holographic weapons sight mounted on the shotgun I used to kill the buck in this story.

Here I am dragging a buck from the woods. The exit from the forest with a well-earned trophy is as much a part of the overall experience as every other aspect of the hunt.

Photo by Janet Carter

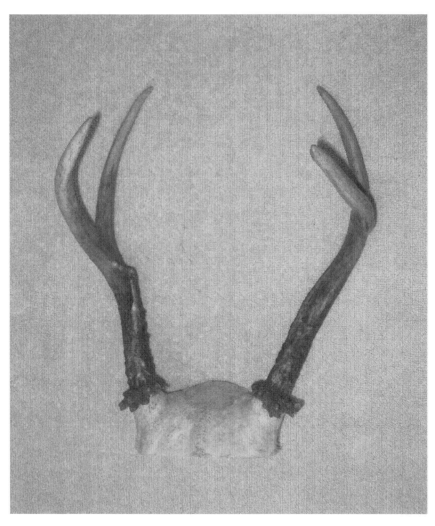

Deeply forked antlers from the yearling buck featured in the story.

FRUSTRATIONS

I'll be the first to admit that things don't always go well in the deer woods. Like everyone else, I've experienced my share of miscues, maladies and misfortune. Some of these doomed interactions with deer could be categorized as self-inflicted wounds, while other failures were dictated by circumstances completely outside of my control. At the time they occurred, I found it very hard to simply laugh any of these bad outcomes away. With the passage of time, however, it became easier to see the humor in many—if not all—of these misadventures. The episodes which continue to irritate are almost universally those where I bear responsibility for the result.

For the most part, I've shared my successes in this book despite the fact that, like any other predator, I fail many more times than I prevail. Truth be told, hunts which conclude with the harvesting of a nice buck tend to offer far more compelling narrative than do hunts that fall short. Nevertheless, I decided to include a few more instances when the outcomes left something to be desired. If nothing else, these stories document the trials and tribulations encountered in real-world hunting, as well as providing the reader some enjoyment at my expense.

This first hunt took place during the Massachusetts muzzleloader season in mid-December. I can't remember the exact year, probably because I'd rather forget the whole affair. John Dupuis and I teamed up for the day. Unfortunately, the conditions were horrible. There was snow on the ground, but a brutal period of freezing rain had top-coated the white under-blanket with a heavy layer of ice.

Conditions were so bad we semi-seriously debated whether to wear hunting boots or ice skates. Joking aside, the woods were very dangerous, as the footing was marginal at best. The only practical way to hunt was by confining our movements to the available well-worn deer runs. Due to the icy crust, walking anywhere else was not only prohibitively noisy but exhausting work, as well. If we had been smart, we would have just stayed home. But, being diehards, John and I elected to give it a go despite our own well-founded reservations and the overwhelming odds we faced.

We entered one of our favorite sections of woods together, before eventually splitting up. If either of us was to realize a shooting opportunity, it would mostly likely come from deer moved by the other or some third party. After our planned separation, I continued to the east along an icy but well-established deer run. I hadn't gone too far when I observed a herd of deer in the hardwoods, well to my front.

When I noticed the deer, I immediately stopped in place and grabbed my binoculars for a better look. Eight or ten animals were milling about in a stand of oaks 150 yards away, alternately walking into view and then disappearing for a period of time. It took me a couple of minutes, but I eventually spied a nice racked buck among the larger group. Unfortunately, I was all but helpless. The buck was well out of range for the equipment I carried that day, and I couldn't move without being detected, mainly due to the abundance of noise which would be produced with each step.

I quickly decided that my only viable option was to wait and hope the buck would work his way towards me. As I continued to keep tabs on the deer from afar, I heard a noise behind me. As I turned to investigate, a doe and her fawn could be seen slinking through the cover fifty yards below me. They were traveling on another deer run which ran parallel to the one I currently straddled.

I froze, doing my best to impersonate a tree, and began praying the duo wouldn't notice me standing there or get a whiff of my scent. Should the newcomers detect me, I was afraid they'd start snorting and blow the whole gig. After what seemed like an eternity, the two bald deer continued on their way.

Once they passed from sight, I felt free to breathe once more. Eager to determine whether the buck was still hanging around, I put my glasses to my eyes and again searched the oak flat to my left. Fortunately, the true target of my attention was still contentedly foraging about for acorns.

By this time, nearly thirty minutes had passed from the moment I first noticed the herd of deer. Yet, nothing had really changed: the buck had moved no closer and I was still glued to the same piece of ground. I had successfully dodged one near-disaster, however. With nothing else to do, I continued my surveillance of the buck using my binoculars, which I deemed to be a pleasant enough task.

My attention was firmly directed towards the buck in the oaks for the next several minutes. For some reason, I decided to check behind me once more. Whether I was simply influenced by the prior passing of the doe and fawn or I sensed a new presence, I'm not sure. When I turned to look, my gaze was returned by a rather large eight-point buck!

The deer was standing in the very same run the previous twosome had occupied, facing me. I had no idea how long the buck had been staring at me. The deer suspected my form didn't quite fit into the larger landscape and he was obviously trying to determine whether I posed a threat.

When I twisted my torso to look behind me, the buck was now in possession of all the information he needed. After a quick snort, the deer bounded directly away from me and disappeared before I could come to my senses, pivot my lower body and raise my gun. As if that turn of events wasn't bad enough, thirty seconds later I heard the disheartening blast of another hunter's muzzleloader from several hundred yards below me, the exact direction towards which the buck had only recently fled.

Sure that someone else had killed the big eight-pointer, I turned my attention back to my remaining prospect. That buck was still where I had last seen him, but ominous changes were forthcoming on that front, also. As I watched through my pocket binoculars, the buck and his remaining companions suddenly came to full attention for a brief moment before bolting off. Seconds later, I witnessed John walk into my field of view.

One minute I was sandwiched between two good bucks, while in the next moment everything was shot to hell. All I could do was shake my head in disbelief. The only thing that offered any comfort was the fact that I really hadn't done anything wrong. Getting a shooting opportunity at the first buck was a long shot from the start. He would have had to move my way at least fifty yards to be within range. I might have had a chance at the second buck if the does had stuck around a little longer or the buck had arrived sooner. I could hardly be faulted for keeping my eye on the first buck. Sometimes, timing is everything.

With both opportunities blown, I was free to check on one last item of curiosity—the fate of the eight-pointer. I picked up the running track and followed it down the hill. Three hundred yards later I encountered a happy hunter standing over the dead deer, confirming the fears I felt upon hearing the gunshot. The buck had a better-than-average set of antlers and looked to weigh approximately 160 pounds. I somehow managed to swallow my disgust, screw a smile onto my face and offer congratulations to the hunter whose luck far exceeded mine on this day.

++++++++

This tale also took place during the muzzleloader season, but in a different location and approximately ten years subsequent to the previous hunt. This time, I was hunting alone during the last week of December. As I recall, a couple of inches of snow covered the ground. While conditions weren't ideal, they were certainly good enough to entertain the possibility of tracking down a buck.

My plan was to look for a buck I had hunted earlier in the season. I had no idea what the deer wore for antlers, assuming they hadn't already been shed, but his track indicated the buck would weigh approximately 175 pounds. From my previous efforts, I was aware of one of the deer's preferred bedding areas. I decided upon a route that would take me to and beyond the thick brushy hill the buck sometimes called home.

As always, I could adapt my plans based upon the sign I encountered. You just never know what might show up. It was possible I would come across an even bigger deer or an enticing setup which accompanied the red-hot track made by a smaller buck. No matter what, I was fairly confident that the large circle I intended to trace would provide at least one viable hunting opportunity for the day.

I parked the truck at a convenient access point for the section of woods I planned to cover and began my hunt. Despite my optimistic outlook, it quickly became apparent that the resident animals had no intentions of cooperating. Fresh deer sign was in abysmally short supply; of that which did exist, none had been deposited by bucks. Nevertheless, I stuck to my strategy. Given the remaining acres of ground I contemplated visiting, I figured it was only a matter of time before I intercepted a track that would be worth following.

Surprisingly, I trudged along all morning without finding the kind of track I had been searching for so diligently. Around 11am, I reluctantly concluded I had picked the wrong spot. I decided to return to the truck and move elsewhere, assuming nothing of note turned up on the way back. I was within a half-mile of my vehicle, pretty much resigned to the fact that I had wasted the entire morning, when I suddenly noticed a deer standing eighty yards in front of me, at the crest of a small hill.

I stopped, straining to see if the new arrival carried any antler. As I carefully surveyed the deer's head, a second deer appeared from below the first. Both animals appeared to be good-sized specimens. My binoculars could have helped me determine whether either deer had horns, but I didn't feel the already tense animals would have tolerated further movement on my part. Apparently, the two deer and I had stumbled into each other as we approached the very same hill top from opposite directions.

Our impromptu standoff lasted approximately thirty seconds, whereupon the antsy duo decided to slink away. As the first deer turned and started walking, I was finally able to visualize the very antlers that had heretofore evaded my detection. By the time I was able to raise my gun to my shoulder, however, the buck had stepped below the crest of the knoll, leaving me without a shooting opportunity. Given the time of year, I assumed the second deer was also a buck, although I never viewed his head.

I immediately took after the duo on a dead run, hopeful that they might stop after distancing themselves from the hill where we crossed paths. I saw the two deer a second time, but they were well in front of me and running hard, leaving me without an opportunity to shoot. At this point, I knew my immediate chance of killing one of the deer had passed, so I stopped to consider my options.

I wanted the deer to settle down before I pursued, so I had time to examine the tracks. At the conclusion of my perusal, I deduced both deer to be $2^1/_2$-year-old bucks. The deer were presently headed up the mountain, utilizing a fairly steep incline littered with boulders and rocky outcroppings. I figured once the bucks reached the top, they would be ready to bed down. Undoubtedly, the animals would choose a location that offered a birds-eye view of their recently laid back-track.

I had the advantage of knowing the country well. The area I anticipated the deer would use as their bedding place was part of a larger convex bowl. The lower elevations didn't offer much in the way of ground suitable for bedding purposes; it was the rim country which was appealing. Rather than following the tracks straight up the incline, where I'd likely be detected before I was within shooting range, I reasoned that my best chance would come from walking along the bowl's rim, keeping the wind in my face as I advanced towards the bucks' expected location.

I waited about thirty minutes before starting my stalk. Whereas the bucks had headed due north, I swung well to the west before I started climbing. The going was steep, but I took my time so that I wouldn't become overheated. I didn't want to become sweaty and then be forced to stand in place for a long time, waiting on some unforeseeable contingency. Once I reached the rim of the bowl, I began working my way eastward, searching for the bucks as I cautiously advanced. I knew that, eventually, I'd either come upon the deer or cut their tracks.

I continued several hundred yards along the ridge. As I cleared an obstacle, a bedded deer popped into view about 100 yards further down the rim. I didn't immediately see the second deer. I quickly sat down in the snow in order to minimize my profile, and brought my binoculars to bear. It was painfully clear that the buck was missing both antlers, his crown replaced by healed over sockets. It didn't take me long to locate the antlered buck, which was standing in thicker cover twenty yards behind the first deer.

The two bucks seemed entirely content and they were ignorant of my nearness. Even so, I found myself in a fairly open spot, eliminating any possibility of moving closer. If I was to shoot, the attempt would have to be taken from my present location.

Although I was at the same elevation as the deer, a significant drop-off separated us. Because of this chasm, the bucks were unusually visible, especially given the distance between us. Had I been viewing them over a similar stretch of level woodlands, the deer wouldn't have been nearly so obvious. At the time, I didn't fully comprehend the implications of such a set-up.

I carefully aligned the front bead on the antlered buck's chest as I simultaneously centered the aiming reference in the rear peep sight. After the gun discharged, I looked up to assess the reaction of the two animals. Shockingly, there was no change in posture, none at all!

More than a little puzzled, I got to work prepping the gun for another shot. With the muzzleloader ready to go, I carefully steadied myself for the follow-on effort. When the smoke cleared in the aftermath of this second attempt, my quarry remained as he had been—completely unscathed.

Since the deer hadn't moved at all, I figured I must have missed big instead of small—twice. I certainly wasn't pleased with my marksmanship, and I was equally at a loss to provide a sound rationale for my shortcomings. Nonetheless, I was willing to keep shooting as long as the buck would accommodate me. As I was loading the smoke-pole for a third attempt, however, the animals finally decided they'd had enough. Without fanfare, they simply walked up the hill and out of sight.

In both cases, I felt I had executed well enough to hit my target, but the buck's indifference indicated something had gone seriously awry. I was more than a little curious as to where my bullets had ended up. When I reached the deer's location, I scoured the area for cut hair and blood drops. Not unexpectedly, I found neither. Since my bullets hadn't reached their mark, I then turned my attention to finding some clue as to where they had struck. Still, I was unable to locate any furrows in the snow or scarred trees in the vicinity of where the buck had been standing.

Suddenly, it dawned on me that my slugs may have been waylaid well before they reached their intended target. The gulf that separated me from the deer contained a full complement of mature trees. As I described earlier, the deer was very visible to the eye, but that didn't mean I had an open path to the buck's chest. Necessarily, I had been shooting through the canopies of the trees which were rooted at the bottom of the hollow. The web of fine, and seemingly innocuous, branches may have been a more serious impediment to bullet flight than I had first imagined.

I turned my attention skyward, as I searched the upper reaches of the trees in the depression for some sign of damage. Eventually, I found one small hanging branch that had been partially severed by a bullet, confirming my hypothesis. I could never find evidence of a second such occurrence, but I was left believing that both rounds had been similarly deflected, some fifty yards prior to reaching the buck.

With the mystery apparently solved, I tracked the bucks until the lateness of the day forced me to turn back. I never saw the two again. Despite the fact that I apparently had a valid excuse for my two errant shots, I couldn't help but feel I hadn't done my very best. Whether or not these feelings were justified, I was left with the sense that I could have shot better, done more or pursued a slightly different course of action, something which would have resulted in me tagging that buck.

++++++++

This final hunt took place sometime in the 1980s, also during the December primitive firearms season. The equipment I carried was pretty pathetic, especially when measured against the black-powder firearms of today. I was forced to shoot round balls from a smooth-bore barrel. Just enough snow covered the ground to enable me to effectively track deer. According to the hunting regulations in effect at the time, a single deer of either sex could be lawfully taken.

I planned on hunting alone, choosing an area dominated by red oak trees. I figured the deer would be frequenting the oaks in an effort to scoop up the remnants of the heavy acorn crop the trees had borne on this particular year. Although deer sign existed, I wandered all over the mountainside for most of the morning without finding tracks that were compellingly fresh. Apparently, I was a day or two late to the party, and the deer had moved elsewhere.

I kept at it, figuring I'd eventually discover where the local herd had relocated. Later in the morning, as I was making a swing through some thicker cover lower on the hill, a doe and a very respectable antlered buck materialized out of the brush to my front. At the time, I wasn't dogging any tracks, so I must have stumbled upon the duo by accident. Presumably, the deer had been bedded before being roused by the noise I made as I approached.

By the time I noticed them, the two animals were standing and staring at me from nearly 100 yards away. Due to the thickness of the cover, all I could see were their heads and necks floating above the brush. As best as I could tell, my prospects for a good shooting opportunity weren't about to get any better. I could fire at the buck's neck or I could let him walk. I decided on the former course of action.

Using the iron sights, I fine-tuned my aim until I was satisfied. Nevertheless, when the thick haze produced by the ignition of the black powder cleared, the deer were still in place. Apparently, my shot had missed cleanly. As I started to re-arm the muzzleloader, the two simply walked away towards the south, showing very little in the way of apprehension or alarm. Once the deer cleared the thick patch they had been standing in, I was able to observe them casually walk single file through the hardwoods for an additional 100 yards, the big buck in the lead.

I finished my work and, gun reloaded, went to check for blood or hair where the buck had been standing. Based upon the deer's reaction I didn't expect to find a thing, but it would have been very poor practice not to have searched. As expected, my examination failed to yield any evidence that my bullet had hit its mark, but the effort couldn't be considered a waste of time. It's always better to operate on hard facts rather than suppositions. Since the deer had left in a very leisurely manner, I deemed my chances of catching them a second time to be quite good.

The duo was headed to the south. Shortly after I took up the track, they entered a piece of land that featured a series of parallel finger ridges which sloped down the hill to the west. In my mind, this terrain was nearly ideal for my purposes. As I approached each ridge-line, I would poke my head above the crest just enough to check out the adjoining valley for sign of my quarry. Finding none, I would then hurry across the depression and up to the next ridge, where I would repeat the process.

If I had gotten on the tracks a little sooner, I might have caught the deer in a vulnerable position in one of these hollows. As things turned out, I navigated this series of undulations without encountering the pair, which continued to behave as if they hadn't a care in the world. Beyond the ridges the terrain flattened considerably and the vegetation changed from mostly hardwoods to a mixture of hard and softwood species.

I slowed my pace and continued to carefully trail the deer into this new, less open section of woods. As I emerged from behind a pine tree I immediately recognized a deer standing seventy yards away, up the hill and slightly to my left. It was the doe, and she had no clue that I was so close. I was sure the buck was nearby, but I didn't dare move. As hard as I tried, I just couldn't locate him from my present location.

A deer of either sex was fair game. Had the hunt occurred twenty years later, I most likely would have held out for a chance at the buck, even if that meant I would return home empty-handed. At that time, however, very few notches had been carved into my gunstock, and the proverbial bird in the hand held a lot more appeal than the one in the bush. I decided to take the doe before that opportunity slipped from my grasp.

I cocked the hammer on the Renegade without making a sound and refined my aim, careful to avoid a four-inch tree guarding the doe's shoulder. I had a relatively easy shot at a stationary target—or so I thought. At the gun's bark, the doe whirled and ran off. As the recoil subsided, I briefly glimpsed the buck do the same. He had been bedded out of sight just up the hill from where the doe had stood. In a split second both animals were gone and the woods were once again silent.

Both my hold and trigger control had been good, and I expected it would only be a matter of time before I collected the doe. As I finished reloading the muzzleloader, however, I noticed something that hadn't been there a minute earlier. The shiny sapwood of a small sapling practical leapt forth from the otherwise dull background where the doe had been standing. My subsequent investigation revealed that the one-inch tree, which was located two feet in front of the deer, had been struck dead center by my ball!

The sapling had been previously bent by some unknown force and now ran parallel to the ground. At the time I pulled the trigger, I didn't realize the small tree was covering, if ever so modestly, the doe's vitals. Hell, I wasn't even able to see the offending stalk from my vantage point. If I had, it's doubtful I could have aimed "around" it, anyway. This miniscule tree-in-waiting was just another hazard to accurate bullet placement, one we confront all the time in the woods.

Despite the fact that the woody stalk had absorbed most of the projectile's punch, I did notice a drop of blood at the scene of what I now considered to be a crime. An occasional red spot could be seen as I followed the twosome another three hours. I managed to garner one more glimpse of the deer—but no shot—before I was forced to call it quits for the day. In all this time, the doe seemed none the worse for her injury. I doubt she incurred little more than a minor flesh wound, and I had every expectation she'd be fully healed within two weeks.

As far as I was concerned, that damn sapling cost me a deer. After the conclusion of the hunting season, I returned to the place where my efforts had been so cruelly thwarted. If I couldn't have the doe, I could claim the tree which saved her. And so, I used a hand saw to remove the section of the tree which bore the scars of my round ball. I never felt it was an equitable trade-off, but at least I had something to show others, as well as to remind me that close only counts when using horseshoes or nuclear bombs.

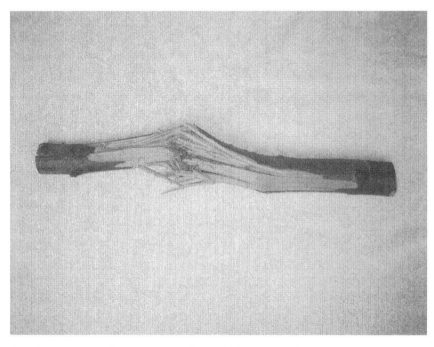

Here's that dastardly one-inch sapling which cost me the doe in the story. My round ball hit almost dead center, losing most of its energy in the process.

THE MISSING WATCH BUCK

This story involves my oldest son Kevin. Once he went away to college, his interest in hunting deer waned, replaced by other pursuits. However, during those years in which Kevin was of legal age and before he graduated from high school, he often accompanied me during the deer season. It was on one such occasion in 1995 that this particular hunt took place. Besides the two of us, my dad and Al Cady were the other participants. Windsor was normally the focus of our efforts, especially during the shotgun season. And so it would be on this day.

Hunting is very much a sport that embraces and upholds tradition. Kevin's addition to the ranks embodied the fourth generation of deer hunters in my lifetime, all of whom considered Windsor to be home turf. Thirty years earlier, I had cut my proverbial hunting teeth not only under the tutelage of members of my father's generation, but also in the presence of the remaining survivors of the generation immediately preceding his. I hunted with Henry Estes (Ken's father), his brother Raymond and Billy Drew. I listened intently to recounted stories of ancient hunting glories and comedies, some of which dated to the 1910s. I could only assume this hunting genealogy was able to trace its roots even further back in history, well beyond my experience and the twentieth century.

As was customary, our group would stake out a piece of woods that we were familiar with, post some members along travel corridors frequented by deer and send the remaining hunters through the cover in hopes of moving the quarry to the standers. Since my ascension more than a decade earlier, some refinements had been implemented. In most of the areas we hunted, I could be counted upon to thoroughly thrash the entire area, without assistance, especially when snow was present. Other hunters considered me to be a deer-jumping machine, which I readily accepted as high praise.

I don't recall exactly where the four of us hunted that December morning, but we undoubtedly followed the aforementioned strategy. Despite having a few inches of snow to work with, we didn't enjoy much in the way of success. As was also tradition, we then broke for lunch. It has always been my belief that, for everyone but me, this was the most-anticipated part of the day's outing. I would have preferred to just continue hunting.

For the afternoon session, I selected an area we hadn't hunted that morning. With the others positioned in supposedly advantageous spots, I began my search of the adjacent cover. Late in my excursion, I jumped a good buck from his bed in a thick alder swamp. I heard but didn't see the deer as he fled. As I followed the running buck, I could actually smell him. That's not a common occurrence, but it often indicates the rut is still in full force. Bucks get pretty rank at that time of year.

Instead of heading towards my cohorts, the buck took a route to the north. When he jumped a dirt road bordering the area we had been concentrating on and disappeared in the next block of woods, I left the track. Now that I had a buck on his feet, I figured we could regroup and quickly redeploy to this new area.

As I walked down the road, I was surprised to discover a second track headed in the same general direction, about 200 yards from the first track. Both sets of prints had definitely been made by bucks; they were of similar size; and they were both exceptionally fresh! I wouldn't learn where the second buck had come from until well after the afternoon's hunt was over.

Our chances were getting better by the minute. The remaining obstacle was time. It was about 1:30pm, but I still had to gather everyone up and send them elsewhere. I had a strategy all mapped out. If all went well, the standers would find themselves well beyond where the bucks had stopped.

But, getting to this location couldn't be done on foot; my partners would have to use a vehicle. I estimated this shifting of resources would take about an hour, and only then could I start on the track. On the plus side of the ledger was the fact that the country the bucks had entered wasn't very big and it contained a narrow pinch-point that constituted an ideal place to ambush the deer, assuming they hadn't already passed through. Realistically, given the time constraints, the impending effort could best be described as hit-or-miss.

There was one surprise I hadn't anticipated. Out of the blue, Kevin expressed a desire to track one of the bucks. He practically begged me to let him take a track. Kevin had never done this before, so I was primarily concerned with his welfare. I didn't want to put him in harm's way or get him lost. My wife would have never forgiven me.

However, for a first-time tracker, the area containing the two bucks was ideal: it was small and it had well-defined borders. Better still, I was able to provide explicit instructions that would help guide Kevin regarding what to do under the most-likely scenarios. I would be nearby and both Al and my father would be in front of him. After thinking the situation over very carefully, I decided to acquiesce to Kevin's request.

While we waited for our elders to reach their stands, I continued to drum my detailed instructions into Kevin. When I felt enough time had passed, we each started on a separate track. I selected the westernmost one, figuring that would serve to further protect Kevin from wandering off course. If he happened to cut my track he would know enough to follow it to me, and not head further west.

As luck would have it, all my instructions, while prudent, were for naught. About 200 yards into our tracking effort, the two sets of prints converged. That didn't necessarily mean the two bucks were traveling together, as there was no way of knowing exactly when each deer had passed through.

I felt somewhat relieved that Kevin was no longer on his own. We quietly followed the two bucks together, with me in the lead. The deer were headed exactly where I had hoped they would go. If the bucks remained in the cover between us and my father and Al, I was increasingly optimistic that someone was going to see at least one of them.

Kevin and I continued on another 300 yards before the tracks led us to a substantial brook. After safely crossing the water, the two of us had advanced less than 100 yards when I noticed something quite unexpected. One of the bucks made a sudden turn towards our left, while the other continued straight ahead.

The source of my curiosity wasn't that the bucks had gone separate ways. Rather, it was related to the lay of the land. The waterway we had just traversed emanated from a series of beaver dams and swamps, which I knew were currently covered in ice.

The buck which had veered to the left was largely surrounded by these natural obstacles. Deer avoid ice at all costs, so I was certain the buck couldn't find a way through the maze. The only way out of the predicament, in my estimation, was for the deer to come back through the general area Kevin and I presently occupied. Since we hadn't yet discovered any sign to that effect, that meant the buck was confined to a very small area and he was most likely still there!

It didn't take me long to analyze the problem and formulate a game-plan. Of course, I had no way of knowing exactly which path the buck would choose to exit his confines, but I decided to leave Kevin right where he was. The area was relatively flat and open, which would provide good visibility and decent shooting conditions. Given all possible options, I fully expected the buck to come back through this area when I rousted him. I just hoped the deer was close enough to my son that he'd have a realistic opportunity.

I also knew this effort wasn't going to take very long. Things were either going to happen quickly or they weren't going to happen at all. I positioned Kevin as best as I could, and gave him instructions to wait and watch for ten minutes, alert to the possibility of the buck coming his way. If he saw neither the deer nor me by then, he was to follow the other track until he met his grandfather. Confident that I had done all in my power to best use the situation to our advantage, I started on the track as quietly as humanly possible.

It was now 3pm and the day was overcast, which meant that it would be getting dark soon. I was creeping along, looking for the deer at each step. I hadn't gone 100 yards when I heard the buck jump from his bed in a small patch of middle-aged spruces. At first, I couldn't see the deer amongst the blackness of the dense trees. As I continued to search for the buck's body, I screamed Kevin's name at the top of my lungs. I wanted to grab his attention so that he would be prepared for the impending action.

My loud warning had barely left my lips when I was able to visualize the buck as he thrashed in the spruces. I instinctively shouldered the shotgun and fired at the jumping deer from fifty yards. The buck came to a sudden stop in a more open section of woods, broadside to me. Obviously hurt by my first shot, I rapidly poured two more slugs into the stationary buck before he settled to the ground.

I made sure the buck was dead and then called for Kevin to come over. This was the first deer kill Kevin had ever been a party to, so he was as excited as I was. That made the moment and the experience special for both of us. It was now 3:30pm, so we had no time to waste if we were to be out of the woods when darkness fell. Plus, I still had to find the other two members of our group. With Kevin's help, I quickly launched into the field-dressing task, explaining what I was doing as I proceeded.

The shortest, best way out of the woods was entirely uphill. Some of the going was fairly steep. Fortunately, the impending effort could be measured in increments of 100 yards rather than miles. Two people made the task more manageable and we arrived at our destination, deer in all, just as it was starting to become dark. As an added bonus to the day, my father and Al drove into view about the same time Kevin and I crested the top of the last hill.

Reunited, we all admired the heavy nine-pointer for some time, as Kevin and I retold our stories. Incredibly, neither of the older guys had heard any of my three shots, and they had no inkling that we had a dead deer in tow until they saw us! Neither one of them ever saw the second buck or his track, either. After retrieving my vehicle and transferring the buck thereto, we all headed back home. The day had been an unqualified success.

Kevin and I stopped at the checking station first, where we learned that the buck was 3^1/$_2$ years old and weighed 158 pounds. Once home, my wife and younger son Andrew were thrilled to hear of our good fortune, as they viewed the buck for the first time. Janet had become somewhat concerned because we were so late getting back. It wasn't often that I arrived well after dark. On this occasion, at least, the reason for my tardiness could be attributed to good luck and not something untoward.

This story might have ended here, if not for two additional pieces of information I learned about in the days that followed. The first tidbit involved Kevin, who unbeknownst to me, called Janet aside later that evening. He confided in her that he had lost his watch during the hunt. My wife reassured Kevin that the watch could be replaced and it wasn't a big deal. Then, after the boys were asleep, she came to me.

When I first saw Janet approaching, she appeared as though she was about to burst at the seams. Initially, I had no idea what the cause of this demeanor could be, but I soon found out.

Just before I left Kevin and went looking for the buck, I gave him explicit instructions to wait ten minutes. If I didn't return he was to take up the other deer's track. Well, Kevin took me quite literally—much more so than I had intended—and pulled out his watch so that he could accurately comply with my orders. At some point during the period beginning with my scream and ending with the last shot I fired, Kevin became so startled that he tossed the watch aside. Once the excitement had passed, he was never able to find the timepiece in the snow, despite some frantic searching. Kevin had withheld this information from me, fearful that I'd be upset with him and that the watch's disappearance would subtract from the day's events.

The final piece of news would take much longer to make its way to me, and it involved where the second buck had come from. It seems that another hunter, I'll refer to him as Mr. W., had encountered the deer well south of where we were hunting at the time. In fact, the buck was in the process of mating a doe when Mr. W. walked onto the scene. Despite the buck's vulnerable position, W. figured he was still fair game (as would have I) and promptly fired at the lovelorn animal. His slug failed to connect even though the distance was quite reasonable. Both deer ran off before W. could shoot again.

Mister W. couldn't imagine how he had missed such an easy target. Search as he might, however, he was never able to find any evidence that the buck had been hit. W. followed the big buck until it crossed a large brook which separated the area he had been hunting from the one we occupied at the time. Then, W. turned back.

Having second thoughts, W. returned to the place where he had witnessed the buck and doe mating, certain that he must have missed some crucial piece of evidence. As he thoroughly re-scoured the area, W. looked up to see a smaller buck staring at him. Alas, this second opportunity turned out no better than had the first. In the space of an hour, two easy, standing shots at different bucks missed their marks.

As might be expected, this unfortunate series of events severely upset W. Rare is the hunter who can't empathize with him. If the rumors can be believed, the next audible sound was the rotor-like whirring of a helicopter in flight as W.'s shotgun spun end over end through the air. In all candor, I've been tempted a few times myself.

Whether I killed W.'s buck or the one I jumped in the alder swamp, there's no way of knowing for sure. As I have stated, both tracks were very similar in size, so much so that I couldn't discern a difference. However, for what it's worth, I do offer this observation: The buck I shot acted very much like he wasn't intimately familiar with the area where I jumped him. I thought the buck, uncharacteristically and needlessly, boxed himself into a situation with too few viable escape options. Whether the reason for doing so could be attributed to brain fog brought on by the rut or lack of familiarity with the terrain is anyone's guess.

Finally, at the time, I expected that if either of us were to shoot at the buck, it would most likely be Kevin. Obviously, I was wrong. In retrospect, I've always felt that I owed this buck, in large measure, to Kevin's presence. By posting him where I did, the buck's already limited choices for extricating himself were reduced further. Had the buck been aware of Kevin, which is a distinct possibility, it might have resulted in a split second of indecision, giving me the edge I needed to kill the deer.

One thing is certain: If Kevin hadn't been with me that day, there would have been nothing to block the buck's retreat in that direction. In that event, I most likely wouldn't have seen the deer long enough—or well enough—to even shoot at him. The buck would have gotten away. Sometimes it pays to have a little help.

My son Kevin standing next to a large rubbed tree a few years prior to teaming up for the buck in this story.

A deer's urine pattern can be used to identify gender. In this photo, there are two tell-tale clues. The urine stream has melted a clearly defined, one-inch circle in the snow, typical of a buck. Better still, this circle is located forward of the rear hooves. A doe urinates behind the rear hooves and the urine covers a larger area.

The State's metal seal along with two slugs recovered from the buck.

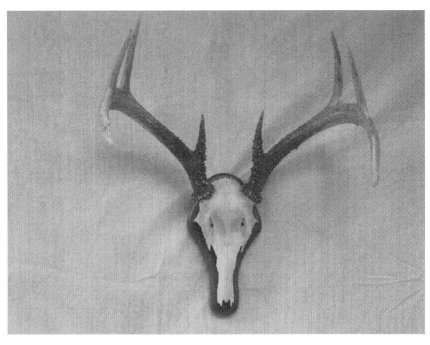

The "Missing Watch" buck I took with my son Kevin. The deer has nine points in total and he weighed 158 pounds.

THREE SHOTS AND YOU'RE OUT

The 2013 shotgun season had just ended. The second week had been pretty kind to us, as there was good tracking snow for the entire week. I was instrumental in getting three bucks killed over that six-day period, but I still hadn't taken one for myself. I managed to track bucks into my son Andrew and John Dupuis' nephew, Mike Shea, early in the week. First thing Friday morning, John and I went to Windsor, ostensibly, to retrieve and drag a buck a friend had shot at last light the previous day. Unfortunately, the buck wasn't hit as hard as we had expected, and the effort turned into a three-hour, four-mile tracking job before I was finally able to finish off the wounded deer.

Up next was the commencement of the muzzleloader season. We received more snow on Sunday, leaving a total of at least a foot on the ground for Monday's opener. Except for the depth, which was about twice what I would have preferred, the snow was perfect for tracking in every other aspect. The white blanket was dry, fluffy and exceptionally quiet to walk in. I was understandably optimistic about my chances of killing a deer.

John Dupuis met me at my house and off we went for the day. Coincidentally, John was celebrating his birthday. We discussed our options and decided to hunt a place the deer and turkeys had been pounding all fall. The reason for all the attention was the beechnuts found there in abundance. John had his preferred spots to stand and he selected one of them. I had my own thoughts regarding where I might best find a good buck track, so I entered the woods in a different location.

It didn't take me long to appreciate the fact that it was going to be difficult to navigate in the woods this day. A couple of days earlier I was practically running over the countryside. With the additional snow, I wouldn't be able to cover nearly as much ground and the walking was going to require much more effort. I would just have to accept the new reality and hope the deer felt equally constrained and burdened.

I hadn't been in the woods an hour when I intercepted just the kind of track I was looking for. Although the sign wasn't smoking-hot fresh, it definitely belonged to a big buck. I estimated the deer's weight at 170 pounds, give or take. Better still, the buck was traveling alone. It's always encouraging to find a good buck early in the day, and I prefer hunting a single animal. Two bucks together is a welcome scenario, also. I just don't like it when a buck mixes with a bunch of does and fawns.

I traipsed along the track, which eventually straightened out and headed north. A half mile later, as the buck approached the stand of productive beeches, I started seeing more deer sign. At first it was just two deer; a hundred yards later, three more tracks appeared. Eventually, I suspected that approximately ten different animals had been frequenting the area, including two other smaller bucks. Finally, there was so much sign it was impossible to keep the buck separate from the rest of the deer.

The problem wasn't just one of numbers. The animals were milling around, depositing a tremendous amount of sign in the process. It was impossible to follow any particular deer in this environment, so I had to start making semi-circles along the outer boundaries of the tracks, as a means of determining where the big buck was traveling.

Actually, this process was one of elimination. By walking in untouched snow on either side of the concentrated sign, I could look for the buck's track exiting the larger group. If I failed to see the big deer's track, I knew he was still within my self-imposed corridor. If other deer crossed my path, I could examine those tracks and dismiss them, leaving me with that many fewer deer to be concerned with. Eventually, I'd be left with a manageable amount of sign, including the big buck's track.

That's how it's supposed to work anyway. Not surprisingly, I was spending a lot of time looking at the ground and not enough searching the brush for deer. Whether I failed to see deer that I should have, or the breeze gave my presence away before I was within visual range, I don't know. In any event, running tracks were suddenly everywhere. Most of them dove off a steep hill to the east.

Despite clear evidence that I had bumped a bunch of deer, I continued making my swings before deciding on a definitive course of action. I needed to be able to account for all the deer in the vicinity, especially the two other deer I believed were bucks.

Eventually, I came to the following conclusions: The big buck that I initially had been tracking was among the herd of does and fawns that ran off to the east. Two additional deer had proceeded north through the maze of tracks. I was almost positive that these tracks belonged to a pair of yearling bucks.

After evaluating my options I elected to pursue the young bucks, at least for the time being. These deer were as yet undisturbed, and it was possible that they would ultimately head towards John. On the other hand, the bigger buck had a lot of company (all of it bald); I'd already spooked him once; and the area to which he fled was away from John. Furthermore, as far as I could tell, this particular block of woods offered me no foreseeable advantages, just negatives.

Not unexpectedly, sorting all the sign present took a long time. In total, I burned more than an hour compiling information before I was able to decipher the whereabouts of every animal and form the conclusions I did. The work was tedious and tiring but essential. In the end, I still had good prospects and it wasn't yet noon.

By all indications, the two young bucks still weren't aware that I was in the area. Of course, that could change at any moment. Based upon my knowledge of this section of woods, I suspected the deer might be bedded not too far ahead. Therefore, I decided to follow at a slow pace, deliberately looking for the deer at each step. Actually, the snow depth was impacting my speed considerably, but I consciously chose to proceed cautiously.

I crept forward another 100 yards. As I cleared some thick beech whips, I immediately recognized a deer's form lying under a small hemlock tree eighty yards away. By the time I saw the deer I was pretty much in the open, although I was no longer moving. Fortunately, the deer was looking elsewhere and didn't notice me. I immediately grabbed my pocket binoculars in an effort to confirm my expectation that the deer possessed antlers. No matter how hard I tried, I just couldn't identify the requisite headgear, as the deer's head was effectively screened by the lower branches of the tree.

My only option to improve my vantage point was a move to my left, where the brush was thick. I feared I'd make an errant sound that would alarm the still-relaxed deer, and there was no guarantee I'd be able to see antlers from my new location.

As an alternative, I could bypass the beech saplings and make a larger swing to my left, but two other potential problems accompanied that course of action. I didn't yet know the resting spot of the second deer, and that animal might detect me as I executed so large a move. Plus, I would have to circle far enough that I would lose sight of the bedded deer, causing me to approach blindly. If I was a bit off, I might stumble into the deer, forfeiting the advantage. Finally, the wind was favorable from my present position, but I couldn't count on it remaining so once I relocated.

Waiting didn't seem like a viable alternative, as it was too cold to stay motionless for any length of time, and it was unlikely the deer would rise any time soon. I decided to shoulder my gun and walk straight at the deer. I hoped that I would see antlers as the presumed-to-be buck turned my way upon noticing me. I was betting that I'd have enough time to identify antlers, aim and fire before the deer bolted away.

I managed to slip a couple of steps closer before the buck picked up on the motion. However, I still couldn't positively see horns and, therefore, I couldn't justify pulling the trigger. Besides that, the deer was up and gone in a split second, anyway. Shortly after the bedded deer disappeared from view, I saw a piece of the second deer briefly, as it ran through an opening. That deer had apparently bedded just beyond the first one.

As I stood there, I felt like I really should have been a little more patient. Some of the options I had dismissed only minutes earlier were beginning to look a lot more appealing with the advantage of hindsight. It's really difficult to "out draw" a whitetail deer. These magnificent animals are practically made from springs, and their reflexes are impressive. I had given myself an almost impossible task to perform. Next time, I'm pretty sure I'll try something else.

I looked at both beds carefully, with the objective of finding some additional evidence that would support my theory that I was dealing with yearling bucks. After all, I had no definitive proof to this point in time. The fluffy snow hadn't allowed me to see a clear imprint of either animal's hoof, which would have helped immensely. However, the snow under a bedded deer gets compressed and warmed. If the deer subsequently steps on the newly melted snow, a well-defined imprint is often left behind. In addition, deer frequently urinate in bedding areas. The pattern of the urine can also be used to identify an animal's gender.

On this occasion, I wasn't able to discover anything conclusive, however. The two deer ran towards the north, which meant that John might still get a chance to see them. I didn't expect the duo to bed again for at least a mile. I also knew I would have to work my rear end off before I received a second opportunity, if that even happened. Walking in the deep snow continued to drain energy and test my mental resolve.

It wasn't long before I felt like I knew where the two deer were headed. Basically, they were following the hill's contour, which meant that, eventually, the deer would swing to the west. With any luck, John would be in position to intercept the pair. I steadily plodded along behind. Fortunately, this expanse of woods hadn't been visited by any other deer, so I could concentrate on seeing deer rather than sorting tracks.

The deer maintained a steady running pace. Apparently, this was a more efficient way for them to advance through the deep snow than was walking. A mile into the tracking job, I could see John up ahead in the hardwoods. As I came nearer, John said, "I hope you're not mad at me." He then explained that both deer had passed within forty yards. John hadn't pulled the trigger, despite the fact that one animal was a spike-horn and the other a four-pointer. Trust me; if my friend had decided to shoot, one of those bucks was a goner for sure.

I was fine with John's decision and I told him so. He had taken a deer of similar age and size during the bow season. Killing one of these bucks would have cost him his remaining tag, and we still had nearly three weeks left to hunt. At the very least, John's encounter with the deer served to finally confirm the premise I had been operating upon for most of the morning—I had two yearling bucks in front of me.

Breaking out my bag of trail mix, I took the opportunity to rest and refresh. As we visited, I said, "You know where they're headed next, don't you?" The question was purely rhetorical. This was our third or fourth time hunting this very same scenario. In fact, a few years earlier, to the day, John had killed a nice buck in this exact spot. I had jumped that deer in almost the same place where I started the two yearlings. Neither of us knew why the local deer behaved as they did, we just knew how to take advantage of their predictability.

In my mind, the next stop for the bucks was the top of the hill, along a transition zone of mixed woods to the east and evergreens to the west. Of course, it was still possible for them to go almost anywhere, but I was so sure that's where they would end up that I would have made a sizeable wager to that effect. As I previously stated, this wasn't the first time I had tracked bucks over this particular route.

After a little more small talk, it was time to get back to work. John left for another traditional crossing point, in case my analysis proved correct but I failed to kill one of the bucks at our next anticipated meeting. I started anew on the tracks. I slogged along another half mile, with the deer headed in the general direction I had expected. When they reached the base of the hill, one of the bucks swung up through a familiar cut, while the other continued on. I had no doubt that they would both end up in approximately the same place.

It was time to get serious. Rather than follow the bucks up the incline, I immediately abandoned the first buck's track and angled to my left as I ascended. I did this for two reasons. First, rather than approaching from below, I wanted to close the distance to the deer along the same topographical contour. This would give me a better chance of seeing the buck. Second, this tactic would put the wind in my face as I advanced on the area that I was sure held the two bucks.

Once I reached the desired elevation, I started creeping west, towards the transition zone where I predicted I would find the deer. I had carefully worked my way forward about 150 yards when I noticed a deer lying 100 yards in front of me. I quickly stopped and grabbed my binoculars. This time, I was immediately able to identify antlers. The buck was bedded in almost the exact spot I had envisioned an hour earlier.

Although I could see the deer, I didn't have a lot to aim at. Trees screened most of the buck's body, but I had a small window to the animal's shoulder. I also had a tree next to me to help steady my shot. The terrain surrounding me was fairly open, and it didn't seem possible to sneak closer. Therefore, I decided to shoot from my present location.

I refined my aim and sent the bullet on its way. When I recovered from the gun's recoil, the buck was still positioned as he had been before I even pulled the trigger. For a moment, I thought I might have broken his neck. However, a quick peek through my binoculars revealed the buck contentedly chewing his cud as if nothing had happened. Obviously, I had failed in my execution.

I ducked out of sight and accessed the fanny pack containing my spare tools and black-powder components. Once I had the gun back in service, I looked up to see the buck resting peacefully in the same spot. As I examined my options a second time, I suddenly came to the realization that I could close the distance another twenty yards by backtracking and using the undulations of the land and some larger trees to conceal my movement. Since my first shot had missed its mark, this course of action seemed more appealing than attempting a second shot from the same location.

I was able to reach my objective without any difficulty at all. I was now eighty yards from the buck. I also had a large yellow birch tree to my front, and I was situated in a small depression, both of which provided excellent concealment. The only problem remaining was one of target availability. That is, I could see the buck's head and neck and his hindquarters, but his chest was completely blocked by a tree.

Other than returning to my previous position, I could identify no additional possibilities for a change in shooting locations. I wasn't willing to send a bullet towards the deer's butt, so I decided to try and thread the needle and hit the base of his neck. Using the birch tree for support, I carefully aimed and finished my trigger pull when the sights looked right. The gun barked a second time, but the results were no different than they had been on the heels of the first report.

The buck was still in his bed and very much alive. Seconds later, however, he decided to check out these peculiar events that had disturbed his solace. While I was on my knees in the hollow, recharging my muzzleloader for a second time, the buck rose and stared down the hill. After several more seconds, the deer took a few cautious steps in that direction. The wind was still good and the buck's attention wasn't directed towards me, so I hurriedly but quietly finished prepping my gun.

Once I had the black-powder weapon ready for action, I leaned forward and peered from the right side of the tree. The buck was clearly visible, but I needed him to take one more step to have an open path to his chest. I was braced against the tree, looking down the sights with the hammer cocked, when the buck took that step, turning slightly in my direction as he did so.

I'm not sure whether he had finally noticed me or not. If he did, the image didn't have time to register on the buck's brain. By then, the bullet had smashed through his facing shoulder and destroyed both lungs, sending the deer straight to the ground. I was incredibly relieved. I wasn't particularly annoyed about the outcomes of my first two chances, as the shots had been difficult. But, if I had missed that easy third shot, I might have used the next bullet on myself.

Certain as I was that the buck was dead, I still prepped the gun once more, just in case. After gathering my supplies, I then approached the fallen animal. Thankfully, by the time I arrived he had long since breathed his last. As I picked up the buck's snow-covered head, I discovered he only possessed one antler, his right. The left side was broken just above the burr. He may have been a yearling, but he wasn't a small one. I estimated his field-dressed weight at a hefty 120 pounds.

The time was approaching 1:30pm, but the day hadn't warmed much. I couldn't be sure, but it felt like the temperature was still in the upper teens. I got everything ready in preparation for gutting the deer. The last thing I did was remove my coat. I intended to work fast, clean up, and put the jacket back on before I froze. As I commenced my knife work, I did notice one thing: the buck's chest contained an enormous volume of blood. With no exit hole, very little external bleeding and both lungs decimated, the blood loss had almost entirely been internal.

After gutting the deer, I gathered up my gear and started down the hill with the buck. The drag was a fairly easy task. When I approached a convenient pick-up point, I left the buck behind a log and went looking for John. When we finally connected, the first thing out of his mouth was, "You have enough ammunition?" Obviously, he had heard my three shots. After a brief chuckle, I subsequently elaborated on the events that had transpired since our last meeting. Then, it was John's turn to laugh.

This hunt was an interesting mix of things done right and things done not so right. On the plus side, I was forced to sort out a very complex array of sign. I did so efficiently and with great accuracy. Eventually, I was able to determine that a pair of yearling bucks was present and undisturbed, from their tracks alone. I had been able to sneak within shooting range of a bedded buck, not once but twice. Finally, while hunting these deer, every prediction I made regarding their behavior was eventually realized.

However, my decision-making was far from perfect. I probably could have killed one of the bucks at our first encounter, if I had only been more patient. At our second interaction, I had initially dismissed a closer approach, only to find it was possible to shave twenty yards off the distance after I missed a shot. Speaking of shooting ability, that hadn't been perfect, either. The first two shots weren't easy, as I was targeting very small pieces of the whole. Nevertheless, I wouldn't have made the attempts had I not believed I could hit where I was aiming. Still, for some unknown reason, both shots managed to miss their mark.

In the final analysis, I managed to take a nice buck on a day when, perhaps, I didn't entirely earn him. Over the years, I've experienced many other hunts when I seemingly performed to perfection, yet failed to even get a shooting opportunity. Luck, both good and bad varieties, is often allocated randomly, in ways that are hard to fathom at times. In this instance, good luck intervened to overcome any of my personal deficiencies, leading to a successful outcome. Such is the way of the woods.

I'd be remiss if I didn't mention John's role in my good fortune. Certainly, the issue regarding the use of his second tag was real. However, John knew that had he killed one of the bucks, I would have ceased hunting to assist him. He also recognized that I hadn't yet had the opportunity to kill a buck, and that this particular day was ideal for my style of hunting. With two antlered deer in front of me, John unselfishly gave me a chance to finish the hunt I had started, despite the fact that it was his birthday. I'll always be grateful for his friendship and generosity.

After the hunt, I jokingly explained to everyone that I deliberately used the first two bullets to maneuver the buck into a better shooting position. That statement never ceased to elicit raised eyebrows and wry smiles. As far as this hunt is concerned, "three shots and you're out" seems to serve as an appropriate tag line for the day.

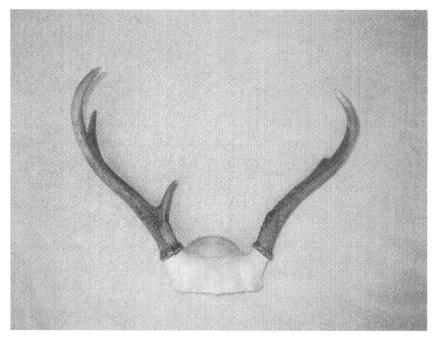

This is the buck I tracked into my son Andrew during the earlier shotgun season. This deer is the biggest yearling I've ever seen, weighing 136 pounds.

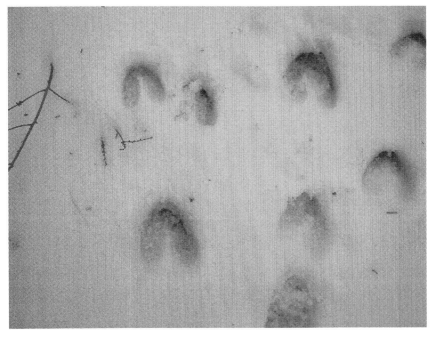

This photo shows where a herd of deer crossed my driveway. Attempting to follow a single animal in the presence of a multitude of sign is painstaking work.

This photo shows deer tracks in a vacated bed. The warmth of the deer's body causes the underlying snow to soften and compress. When the deer subsequently stands, a sharp imprint is often produced, even if the snow is otherwise soft and fluffy.

My Swarovski pocket binoculars. Primarily, I use these to look for antlers on deer I've already spotted with my naked eye.

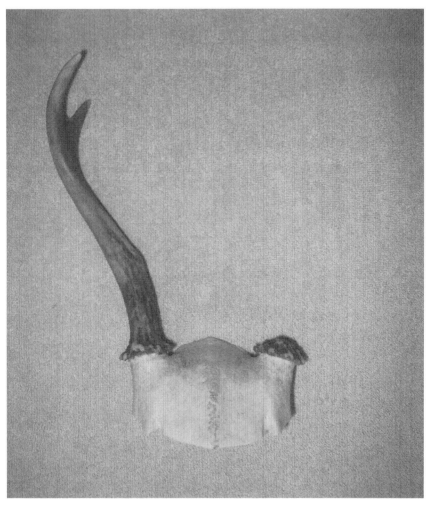

Skilled tracking and some very good luck allowed me to take this yearling buck.

A TALE OF TWO HUNTS

The year was 1996. At that time, the shotgun season in Massachusetts was two weeks long. After that period ended, you could hunt an additional three days with a muzzleloader. This particular story spans both seasons, but it features the same buck. Although the two separate days enjoy similarities of landmarks and topography, they vary in other important ways, notably the buck's behavior and the end result of the hunts.

It was on one of my pre-season scouting forays that I first became aware that a large buck was residing in the vicinity of one of our traditional stomping grounds in Windsor. Specifically, this buck, which I estimated would field dress in the neighborhood of 180 pounds, appeared to be spending a lot of his time behind the Windsor Elementary School and the neighboring Town Garage.

Bucks of this size couldn't be found just anywhere, so I made him a high priority for the upcoming hunting season. As is often the case, though, just because the season is open there is no guarantee that tracking snow will be present. That forces me to pick my spots and track only when it is feasible to do so.

Finally, on the first Saturday of the shotgun season, enough snow was present to justify investing the effort it would take to track this buck down. Although my father and Al Cady were hunting that day, I forewarned them that I intended to "big buck" hunt on this particular outing. I used that term as shorthand for: "If I find a track I like, I'm probably gone for the day." Normally, in conditions not conducive to tracking (e.g., bare ground), I'd try to position other members of our hunting party in good crossing areas and then "push the brush" in hopes of moving deer into stationary cohorts. Obviously, I had other plans for the day.

Besides having the requisite snow on the ground, the day featured intermittent snow squalls and quite a bit of wind. The temperature was in the low twenties. I started my search right behind the schoolhouse, where I immediately discovered the buck's fresh track.

I hadn't followed the sign 100 yards when I saw the buck hurtle out of the bed he had chosen within the thick confines of a stand of alders. He was gone before I could even get my gun to my shoulder. Nonetheless, I was optimistic about the day because it was still early and I had hours of hunting ahead of me. I figured I would get more than one chance at the buck before day's end.

The buck headed south and eventually crossed below the end of a small, grass-covered airstrip cut into the otherwise thick cover. From there, he started working to the west where he jumped across a paved road and into a new and much larger block of forest. I hadn't spent much time hunting in this area, so I didn't know the terrain as intimately as the parcel of ground I was leaving.

That didn't deter me one bit, though. I'd figure out the best way out of the woods when the day ended or once I killed the deer, whichever came first. I carry topographical maps for just this purpose. If you want to be successful while tracking deer, you have to be willing to exceed your comfort level. And, you can't kill a buck if you're constantly worried about where the truck is instead of concentrating on the animal you're hunting.

As best as I could tell, it was me and the buck for the rest of the day and I relished the opportunity. I tracked the deer for another mile or so. By then, it had become quite blustery, a feature of weather which would continue the rest of the day.

While walking through a stand of spruces I was suddenly brought up short by the distinctive but muffled sound of a deer snorting, even as it competed with the much more prevalent noise made by branches whipped back and forth by the wind. The buck was close, but, unfortunately for me, my ears were unable to locate the direction from which the snort had emanated. My eyes were equally useless, as an ill-timed snow squall all but obliterated my vision as I frantically searched for the ghost-like buck.

Naturally, the buck had been bedded close by. I might have had a good chance to kill him under different circumstances, I'll just never know. What I do know is this: After this second encounter the buck became quite wild. He certainly never bedded again. I followed him approximately ten more miles, but he never even slowed down. I never felt that I was anywhere close to the buck over all that distance.

Despite my dogged pursuit for the rest of the day, I never had an opportunity to pull the trigger. Around 4pm, I left the big buck's track where it crossed Route 9, about a mile west of the schoolhouse where I had begun the day. My consolation prize was that my truck was located that same distance up the hill. I'd had a very long day and I was tired, to say the least!

Unfortunately, that was the last opportunity I had to hunt that buck during the shotgun season. On the heels of this adventure a significant ice storm descended on the higher elevations of the county, leaving the trees and the available snow covered in a heavy layer of ice. The landscape was beautiful to behold, but almost impossible to hunt. The coating of ice was thick enough that it almost held my weight. The resulting mix made for exhausting and excessively noisy walking, as well as lousy tracking conditions. As much as it pained me to abandon this deer, I hunted at lower elevations where things weren't as bad, all the while hoping that I'd eventually get a return match.

Much to my dismay, the ice persisted for the remainder of the shotgun season. It looked increasingly unlikely that my luck would fare any better during the muzzleloader season. In fact, nothing had changed over the first two days. However, a significant warm-up arrived on the evening before the final day. With temperatures expected to remain well above freezing, I figured I'd make the trip up the mountain and at least check on the conditions. If the ice had softened as much as I projected, I would go looking for the buck.

My father and Al came along for the final hunting day of the year. Upon our arrival, it was clear that the icy top coat had softened dramatically, as hoped for, so the hunt was on. I gave my elders instructions for potential stand locations and set off in search of the big buck. It didn't take me long to find his oversized hoof print in the softening snow. The sign wasn't exceptionally fresh, so it took me a little while to follow the deer to his bedding spot.

This time, the buck was lying just south of the Town Garage. By the time I jumped him from his bed on this occasion, visibility had become an issue. The warmer-than-normal air mass reacted with the colder snow to produce a fair amount of fog. As a consequence, I didn't even get a look at the buck as he fled his lair. As I diligently followed behind, the fog not only screened my prey but it also made it difficult for me to identify those features of terrain which would tell me exactly where I was at any given moment.

Around 11am, the buck crossed the lower end of the airstrip, which I did recognize, just as he had the first time I tracked him. Rather than push him further, I thought the best course of action was to gather the troops and break for lunch. That would give the deer a chance to settle back down. Since I felt I had insight into the buck's next course of action, I could subsequently deploy my father and Al so that they had a better chance of intercepting the deer during the afternoon hunt.

As we ate our lunch at the local store, I kept commenting on how I'd just like to get a good look at this particular deer. I'd never even glimpsed what the buck had on his head. Al took the opportunity to say, "I'd like to see you standing over him with your knife in your hand!" Naturally, from my perspective, that would be even better. By the time we left the store the temperatures were solidly in the forties and the sun was beginning to burn off the fog. Only a handful of hours remained in the 1996 hunting season.

With the others posted in what I hoped would be productive stands, I picked up the buck's track where I left it. It wasn't long before I had several other deer up and running. Even so, it wasn't difficult to keep the big deer's track separate from the rest. From this point on, I began seeing deer on a regular basis.

For the buck's part, he continued to generally head south and I was anticipating he was about to swing west and cross the road in the vicinity of his previous route some ten days earlier. Instead, the big deer elected to reverse direction, turn northward and remain in this same block of woods, and in the company of the other deer.

Over the next hour, I slowed my pace considerably, as I kept bumping and seeing deer as I progressed. On a couple of occasions, I was sure the deer I caught a glimpse of was the buck I had been following. For whatever reason, he didn't seem to want to go anywhere. That was fine with me; I was willing to play tag for as long as he would accommodate me. If the buck continued this behavior, I figured it was only a matter of time before he made a potentially fatal mistake.

The buck finally distanced himself from the does and fawns. He still seemed to be in no hurry to leave the country, though. After working his way around the backside of a pond south of the airstrip, the big buck then made a turn towards the west. I assumed he was now intent on crossing the paved road, somewhere in the general location of where my hunting partners were stationed.

If that was the deer's plan, he never got there. At the crest of a hill the buck entered a thick stand of smallish hemlocks. Before exiting the conifers I stopped inside the heavy cover to carefully survey the terrain below me. Although the buck's direction of travel was straight ahead, I quickly identified his broadside outline well to my left, about eighty yards away. With the sun low in the sky behind him, the mature buck was almost perfectly backlit, making him very easy to see. All these years later, I can still visualize the setting in vivid detail! The only thing missing from the scene was a sign on the buck's flank reading: "kill me."

Almost without thinking, I raised the muzzleloader to my shoulder, cocking the hammer as I did so. After steadying the sights I pulled the trigger on the cap-lock. The big buck bolted at the shot, apparently well hit. Sometimes when you drill a deer in the vitals, the animal appears to be running faster than physical possible. As I watched the buck run away, he looked like he was moving at full speed and floundering all at the same time.

I took my time reloading the muzzleloader, sure that a second shot wouldn't be necessary but opting to be prepared, just in case. Then I went to where the deer had been standing to search for blood sign. A three-foot-wide carpet of crimson awaited me. The path weaved less than 100 yards to the fallen buck, shot through the heart and completely drained of blood.

I admired the symmetrical eight-pointer for a few minutes and then went looking for my father and Al, who weren't too far away. The three of us then returned to my prize, where Al did get to see me standing over the buck with my knife. The drag to the road was short and sweet for a change, and we were headed back home well before dark. A subsequent visit to the checking station revealed that the field-dressed buck weighed 175 pounds and that he was 6½ years old. I've only shot one other buck that old. It's my strong belief that once a buck reaches four years of age, he's more likely to die of natural causes than from a hunter's arrow or bullet.

I spent two days chasing this worthy opponent, and his behavior couldn't have been more different on the two hunts. There's no way of definitively accounting for those differences, but I do believe deer tend to be spookier on days where gusty winds are present. The bluster present during the first hunt may have made the buck more skittish than normal, resulting in a more protracted chase and an inability to get close to the deer.

I also think that the warm temperatures experienced during the second hunt affected the buck's willingness to exert himself. After all, I don't expect that deer enjoy being hot and sweaty any more than we humans do. Although the rut was long over, the presence of those other deer may have also inhibited the buck from choosing a course of action which involved vastly more acreage. In combination, these two factors may have worked to my advantage, keeping the buck in relatively close quarters over an extended period of time.

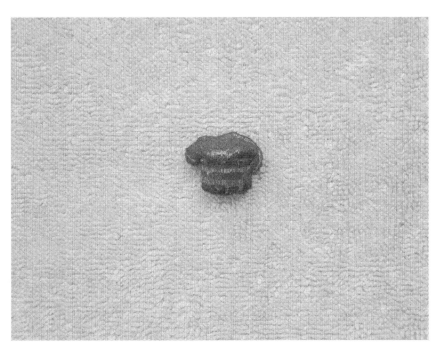

This is the muzzleloading bullet that killed the buck which was the subject of this story. Specifically, this piece of lead is a Hornady Great Plains bullet weighing 425 grains.

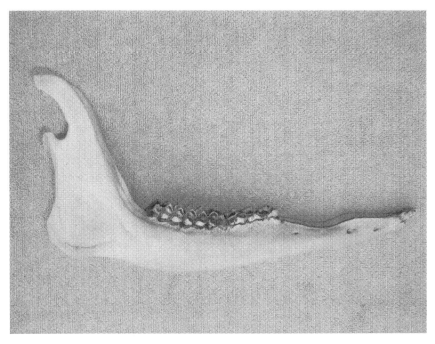

The lower jaw bone taken from the buck. Based upon tooth wear, the Fish and Game people determined him to be 6 1/2 years old.

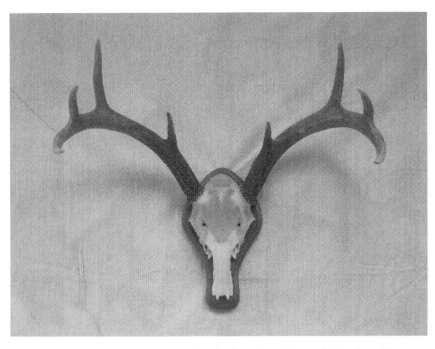

This buck may have given me the slip the first time I hunted him, but things turned out better on the rematch. This buck was 61/2 years old and tipped the scales at 175 pounds.

THE BIGGEST BUCK I NEVER KILLED

Sometime during the 2006 hunting season, my friend John Dupuis discovered signs of a large buck during an excursion into one of our local hunting areas. From his description, this was an animal worth pursuing. So when the conditions were right, the two of us set off to find the deer.

In order to maximize our chances of locating the buck, John entered the woods from one direction while I chose a different route. John intercepted what he thought was the buck's track early in the morning. When I arrived on the scene I made two observations. First, the track wasn't terribly fresh. That wasn't a concern because, all things considered, I felt the deer was most likely not too far away. Second, the track had obviously been made by a very large buck. If an even bigger deer was frequenting these woods, I wasn't willing to give up a sure thing and go look for something I was pretty sure didn't even exist.

John selected a stand in the general area where the track had been discovered, a relatively flat piece of ground dominated by beeches, while I started on the track. The day was very cold (low teens) with gusty winds, which made for even colder wind-chill temperatures and blowing snow.

It didn't take me long to jump the buck and the chase was on. Over the next hour or so, the buck traced a small ellipse which eventually brought him back through the area where we originally picked up his track. Unfortunately, the buck's path through the beech flat didn't quite intercept John's chosen stand location.

By the time round two began it was past noon. This time, the buck elected to make a much bigger swing on a different part of the mountain. I jumped the buck twice during this jaunt but I never saw him either time. Now aware that he had a determined tracker on his trail, the buck was choosing his bedding sites with great care.

Around 3:30pm, after a multi-mile journey, the big buck once again returned to the same area where we initially located him. By this time, however, John had recently vacated the premises. Frankly, I couldn't believe John had been able to stay as long as he had. I was cold and I had been on the move all day! Even patient and prepared sitters like John have their limits.

That evening, I mulled over what lessons I could glean from the day's hunt. First, there was no question this was a big animal. I figured the buck would field-dress in the 190-pound range. If my weight-to-track-size estimate was off by just a little, he might even make it to the prestigious 200-pound mark. Second, for some reason, the buck liked the flat where we first found his track. Prior to being disturbed, he had chosen this place to bed. Even with me hounding him, the buck had twice returned to this same general location. Third, referencing my topographical maps, I made note of how the buck used features of terrain to move about his domain. This knowledge could only help me on subsequent encounters.

After mulling things over a bit, I put together a thoughtful game-plan for the next morning. I believed John's choice of stand locations in the flat offered him the best chance of killing the buck, assuming I could get the big deer on the run again. However, the snow was pretty noisy, so I had some concern about how to get John into position without tipping the buck off.

With these considerations in mind, I thought the best course of action was for the two of us to walk into the flat together. Once John was settled, I would continue on and re-acquire the track where I had abandoned it the day before. That way, any deer within earshot might conclude that only a single hunter had broken the stillness, concealing John's presence to the greatest extent possible.

It's worth noting that I very rarely pick up a track where I left it the day before. That tactic is usually a waste of time and energy. In this instance, however, it seemed like a wise choice. The buck had been on his feet the entire day, so I believed he would be unusually tired and hungry. Once the deer realized I was no longer following him, I figured the buck would feed heavily and rest, electing not to travel very far to do so.

John saw at least some wisdom in my approach, so off we went early the next morning, hopeful for what the new day might bring. Once John was positioned, I proceeded to follow the track beyond where I had retreated some eighteen hours earlier.

I was walking along at a brisk pace when I noticed a decidedly fresh set of the big deer's tracks cross the day-old prints I was fixated upon. This was an unexpected and wel-come turn of events. Less than an hour into the hunt, I had the big buck somewhere right in front of me—undisturbed and oblivious to my presence.

Given the time of day and the freshness of the track, I knew that the deer could still be on the move. At worst, he had recently bedded somewhere up the hill he was slowly ascending. From this point on I slowed to a crawl, meticu-lously searching the brush for the buck with each step for-ward. The tracks led me to a high point which featured a convex rim with a significant drop-off below. As I crept for-ward, I suddenly saw the buck standing below me and to my right, about 100 yards away.

Based solely on the deer's size, there was no doubt this was the animal I was after. However, one very significant problem remained: No matter how hard I tried I couldn't see antlers, even with my compact binoculars. I could see the buck's head, but brush prevented me from positively identifying headgear. As I struggled to make this important determination, the buck laid down while I watched. Despite the buck's change in posture, his new presentation did nothing to improve my ability to see his horns.

The wind was blowing in my face and the deer had no idea I was within shooting range, so I sat down in order to make my wait more comfortable. I figured it was only a matter of time before the buck moved his head enough to allow me to positively confirm the existence of antlers. Then, assuming I hadn't become so cold that I couldn't adequately control my aim, he was mine.

I know some readers might question why I just didn't take the shot. Believe me; I was tempted! However, it was the middle of December and, around here, it's not uncommon for bucks to begin to shed during this time-frame. Generally, the oldest, most mature bucks drop their antlers first. Although the percentages were with me, I just couldn't be certain whether the buck's antlers were still attached to his head or buried in the snow somewhere.

About ten minutes into my sit I unexpectedly felt a momentary shift in the wind direction. His nose suddenly full of my scent, the buck rose to his feet and walked away at a brisk pace. In three steps, and in the span of as many seconds, he disappeared from my sight! I couldn't believe what had just transpired. One moment I was brimming with anticipation and confidence that I was about to kill this great deer; in the next, I felt completely stunned and cheated.

I gathered myself and once again set off in pursuit. The buck walked steadily for approximately two miles. Although he never ran, it was clear to me that he intended to vacate the area for one he deemed more secure. I plodded along behind, patiently waiting for some change in behavior which would signal the buck was about to bed once more.

I was following at a steady pace when I noticed that the big deer had stopped to browse some low vegetation, a sign that quite often precedes bedding down. Almost simultaneously, about eighty yards in front of me, an out-of-place color caught my eye. As I reached for my binoculars to more carefully examine my discovery, the buck bounded from his bed and disappeared. And this time I was able to see antlers momentarily as the buck swapped ends, an observation which only served to make matters worse.

Although I stopped as soon as I saw the signs of feeding, I had taken one step too many. In doing so, I had cleared a small contour of topography which hid my presence from the buck. I'm sure he set up this particular bedding location with that exact intent. Incredibly, I had witnessed this mature buck lying in his bed not once but twice, and on the very same day. Yet, other than the memories, I had absolutely nothing to show for my efforts.

After this encounter the buck turned quite wild. I continued my pursuit for the rest of the day, but the buck stayed pretty much on the run and I never caught another glimpse of him. Eventually, dwindling daylight forced me to leave the track, whereupon I went looking for John. After relaying the events of the day, we headed for home. For my part, I was probably more drained emotionally than physically, given the two close encounters I had experienced. Still, I estimated I had tracked the buck well in excess of twenty miles over the course of these two days.

I had a few more chances to track the buck over the next two weeks. I would have hunted him every day, if that had been possible. However, factors beyond my control limited my opportunities. Sundays are closed to hunting, and on some days the weather wasn't cooperative. All-day snow storms, ridiculously noisy conditions, and the like made for next-to-impossible tracking conditions. A couple of times I couldn't find the buck's track until later in the day, which basically gave me a single chance at killing him—before he exited his bed. By that time, the big deer was choosing these locations with great care, and I came up empty.

The hunting season was rapidly winding down and along with it my chance to tag this great buck. I did enjoy one last encounter with this deer before I was forced to put my gun away for the year. The hunt began when I jumped the buck from his bed at the top of a hill, in an area where he had bedded on a couple of other occasions. As was par for the course, I didn't get a look at him when he left, even though it was reasonably quiet afoot. From there, the buck wove his way south.

I knew the terrain fairly well, but I wasn't exactly sure where I was at all times, mainly because my concentration was almost entirely focused on seeing the deer in front of me. I was trailing the buck along a small brook when I came to a place where the water trickled down a ridge. Although the track was headed in the same direction, something caught my attention off to my left, almost ninety degrees away from where the track was leading me. I quickly identified the object as a deer, standing broadside and facing to the left. I estimated the range to be 100 yards.

I was pretty well exposed, so I couldn't risk moving much. Holding my muzzleloader between my knees, I was able to slowly raise my binoculars. This time, unlike the very first time I tracked this deer, I was able to identify antlers gracing the buck's head.

Although the buck's chest was visible, a six-inch window through the intervening trees was the extent of the path to his vitals. I sure could have used a tree to help support my impending shot, but one wasn't immediately available and I didn't dare risk moving the few steps it would take to access one. I was just going to have to take the shot off-hand.

I steadied my aim and when the sight picture looked good, I finished my trigger pull. The buck swapped ends and raced downhill and to the right. In a few bounds he was out of sight. From where I stood, I didn't have an impression as to whether or not the deer was hit. In my mind two possibilities existed: the buck was likely dead just out of sight, shot through the lungs, or my bullet hit a tree.

I recharged the black-powder gun and headed to where the buck had been standing, anxious to learn if I had connected. A cursory look for hair and blood came up empty, imparting a sinking feeling in my heart. I followed the jumping tracks another fifty yards or so, but evidence that my bullet had found its mark was still lacking.

Returning to where the buck had been standing, I performed a more concerted search for signs that the bullet had struck a tree. I finally found a small beech tree, about ten yards in front of where the deer had been standing, bearing the scars of my misplaced round and confirming the fears that had been steadily building. Although it was of little consolation, if the slug had only been placed an inch further to the right, I would have surely killed that buck.

It was only after I confirmed that I hadn't hit the deer that I came to fully realize where I was situated geographically. As I fired at him, the buck had been looking at me from the exact same spot he occupied when I first laid eyes on him some two weeks earlier. I hadn't initially recognized the relevant landmarks because the buck had approached the area from a different direction.

Despite my self-inflicted misfortune, I was still hopeful that I'd get another chance at the buck during what remained of the day. But, it was not to be. Many more miles of tracking yielded no additional sightings or opportunities, just sore feet and aching muscles. All too quickly, the hunting season was over. If I was destined to kill this buck, it would have to wait until the following year.

Immediately after the hunting season ended, I returned to the site of my misplaced shot. I wanted to take a picture of the tree I had wounded, but I was also curious about the actual distance between me and the buck. So, I toted my rangefinder. Due to the multitude of trees present, I didn't expect to be able to range the entire shooting distance in one pass. Therefore, I also brought along a large target that would enable me to range in increments. After a little work, I concluded that the shot I had taken off-hand measured 110 yards. To be sure, that's not an easy shot, but it is certainly one that I'm capable of making.

In March of the following year, I was seeking suitable photographs to illustrate a book I was writing entitled— *Tracking Whitetails: Answers to Your Questions.* I went looking for the buck because I wanted to visually document track size and features of gait that a buck of this caliber leaves behind.

As I had hoped, I found the buck and took several images that helped improve the book. Not unexpectedly, I originally located the deer in a slightly different location, at a lower elevation than where I had spent all that time hunting him. However, it's worth noting that as soon as the crusty snow softened, the buck returned to the now-familiar haunts higher on the hill.

All told, I spent more time tracking this buck than any of the others I've encountered. As a result, I felt that I knew a great deal about this individual animal, including preferred bedding areas, travel corridors and where he would go when pressured. I couldn't wait to hunt him again in the coming season.

Alas, it was not to be. My late-winter photographic sessions were my final interactions with this particular deer.

By the time the 2007 hunting season finally rolled around, there was no sign of him or his track in any of the usual places.

It's possible that a bow hunter took the buck very early in the season, but it's unlikely that news of someone killing a deer of this magnitude would have failed to reach me or John. Speaking of John, he killed a buck weighing 193 pounds in the first week of the shotgun season, before the season's first snowfall. Although the location wasn't too far removed (in miles) from where we had hunted the deer the previous year, the big buck never set foot anywhere near this patch of ground in all my time tracking him. In my mind, this raises questions as to whether John killed this particular animal or another.

Whatever the ultimate cause of the big buck's demise, I thoroughly enjoyed the time I spent hunting him. If not for my slightly errant shot, he could have—perhaps should have—assumed a place of honor in my home.

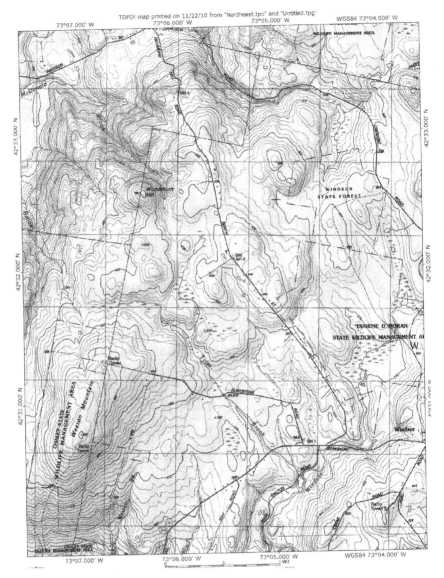

One of several topographical maps I carry while hunting. They keep me from getting lost and help me determine the best way out of the woods once I kill a deer. Plus, they can help start a fire in a pinch.

My Thompson/Center Omega muzzleloader, the gun I used to shoot at the big buck. The reason for missing lies with me and not this firearm, which is quite accurate and dependable.

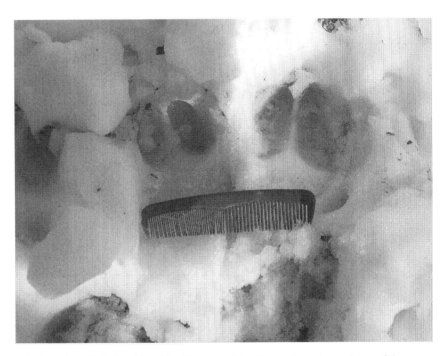

The imprint of the buck's wide, blunt-toed hoof, seen here in moist, melting snow.

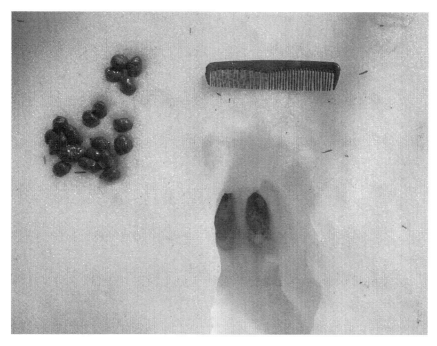

Over-sized hoof print and equally impressive droppings left by the buck.

The big buck's walking track, photographed after the hunting season ended.

This is the small beech tree my bullet struck on its way to the buck. An inch to the right and the deer would have been mine!

John Dupuis and the huge buck he shot during the 2007 shotgun season. Is this the deer I spent so much time chasing the year before? The buck weighed 193 pounds, which fits the bill, but this deer met his demise in a section of woods where I had never before encountered the presence of the buck I missed. I guess we'll never know for sure.

Photo Courtesy of John Dupuis

HUMOR IN THE WOODS

I suppose it's nearly impossible to spend forty-odd years hunting and not accumulate at least a few stories that are down right knee-slappers. Here are several of my favorite laughter-invoking tales.

One year, when my youngest son Andrew was old enough to hunt, we journeyed to New Hampshire together. Andrew's participation in the annual November hunt marked the third generation of Carters to chase deer in these woods. By this time, the hunting crew was shrinking badly. Billy Drew and Bob Donnelly had both passed on to happier hunting grounds and Bill Donnelly no longer hunted with us very often. That left me, Andrew, Al Cady and my father to press on.

One afternoon the four of us were hunting in the vicinity of an old maple syrup operation. In most places, there was just enough snow on the ground to track deer, but it was melting. South-facing slopes were rapidly changing to brown, while shaded and protected areas held more snow.

It was in one of these lower-elevation, out-of-the-way places that Andrew encountered Al at the conclusion of our latest effort to move deer around. And Al had a big problem. Difficulty with his hearing had been an increasingly troublesome burden for him over the course of the last several years. Things had gotten so bad that Al had recently acquiesced to purchasing a set of hearing aids to help restore his failing auditory senses. Although the technology in these modern contraptions is impressive, a quality set of aids is expensive.

Just before Andrew's arrival, Al had bent over to navigate a blow-down, whereupon one of the hearing aids slipped from his ear and disappeared into the nearly two inches of snow that still blanketed this particular location. Our older companion had been searching for the wayward object for several minutes, to no avail. Andrew was eager to help, but Al had just about given up hope of recovering the costly medical apparatus.

As the two of them discussed the problem, Andrew thought he could hear something unusual. After politely instructing Al to be quiet, my son zeroed in on the origin of the noise. The lost hearing aid was emitting the tell-tale feedback squeal that we are all familiar with. Al couldn't hear the high-pitched whine, but the noise was discernible to Andrew, who promptly followed the sound to its source and plucked the missing device from the snow. Greatly relieved, Al said, "Andrew, I could kiss you on the lips."

++++++++

When I first started hunting, Billy Drew epitomized what it meant to be a knowledgeable and successful deer hunter. He had countless deer to his credit, as well as the stories to match. As a teenager in the late 1910s, Billy killed a buck that weighed 286 pounds. Many more would follow, although none would match that bruiser in weight. Until Billy reached seventy-five years of age, no one could keep up with him in the woods. Billy was easy-going, pleasant and he had a dry sense of humor.

He and his wife lived in an old farmhouse in Windsor, and they both liked to hang on to stuff, such as old newspapers, magazines and the like. In modern parlance we might refer to them as hoarders. As might be expected, the home of an older couple which had spent years saving things tended to become somewhat cluttered and disorganized. And so it was at the Drew household.

Every room contained multiple stacks of paper goods, some dating back decades, as well as assorted bags and boxes of other goodies. To an outsider, it was difficult to fathom how the inhabitants knew what resided where. Don't get me wrong; I'm not judging Billy or poking fun at him. We all loved him for the person he was. The only reason I mention Billy's lifestyle is that it is relevant to the story.

One morning during the 1979 shotgun season in Massachusetts, a group of us decided to hunt a small piece of Billy's property. Besides me and Billy, the rest of the party included Al Cady and his wife Joyce, as well as Kenneth and Richard Estes. Billy, Joyce and I were to take positions along the property line, while the other three members of the group pushed towards us from the east.

As is so often the case, deer have an uncanny ability to negate human design for their destruction. As Billy, Joyce and I walked single-file towards our stands, the woods in front of us suddenly exploded with jumping deer. I wasn't sure how many animals we had actually disturbed, but there seemed to be white flags everywhere.

Normally, such an occurrence would be viewed as desirable. However, the herd decided to head west. Instead of being surrounded by our small group, the deer were now outside the box, so to speak.

In light of our unexpected discovery, the three of us talked things over for a few minutes. With that many deer in the immediate neighborhood, it seemed unlikely that the walkers would encounter additional animals. Billy and I thought our efforts would be better directed towards the deer we had just bumped. The odds were long, but we might just get a shot at a deer or be able to turn them back in the direction of the walkers.

We decided to leave Joyce at the upper end of the property boundary. Billy would walk northward until he hit a mowed field. From there, he would swing to the west in an attempt to get in front of the deer. After waiting fifteen minutes, my job was to slowly work my way through the intervening block of woods. If we were lucky, we just might trap the deer between us or push them to Joyce. Snow was absent, so the new plan would be executed without the benefit of tracks to follow.

We placed Joyce in a seemingly advantageous spot, and Billy started on his planned route. I referenced my watch so I'd know when to commence my role in the affair. Five minutes hadn't yet passed when I could see Billy walking towards me. And that definitely wasn't part of the plan. In addition to his premature appearance, Billy's body language was decidedly negative. There was no spring to his step, and his chin was stuck on his chest. I was at a loss to imagine what could have possibly happened in such a brief period of time to precipitate this deviation in game-plan, but I was about to find out.

As Billy approached, he started shaking his head back and forth and muttering about his shotgun. At first, I thought he said he had taken a shot, but it would have been impossible for me not to have heard the gun's report, which I hadn't. Billy just continued ranting about how his gun wasn't working. Piece by piece, additional details slowly dribbled out. Eventually, I began to better understand what had transpired.

Billy had barely reached the field's edge. As he cleared a small rise in the meadow, he saw several deer milling around below him, about seventy yards away. He took aim at the closest animal and pulled the trigger. However, for some unknown reason the gun didn't discharge.

Billy quickly ducked down behind the contour in the field to try and fix the cause of the misfire. As he crouched in the grass, frantically trying to get his shotgun in working order, a big antlered buck stepped into the field about half way between him and the group of other deer. The buck stood there broadside for a minute before trotting away with the whole herd.

Billy was as animated as I had ever seen him, as he kept saying, "I don't have a gun; this one doesn't work." I finally offered to take a look. As I examined the well-worn Ithaca 12-gauge pump gun, I quickly noticed the problem— a 16-gauge shell sat in the barrel just forward of the chamber. I removed the barrel and used a straight stick to push the under-sized ammunition from its confines, chuckling uncontrollably as I did so.

I showed Billy the 16-gauge round and explained what had happened. He then recalled that loading his gun that morning had been problematic. Billy explained that shells kept slipping from the weapon as he tried to fill the magazine. Obviously, at least some of the ammunition my friend had on hand didn't match his shotgun's chambering. A subsequent check later in the day would reveal that the brown paper bag Billy had drawn his ammo from that morning contained both 12 and 16-gauge slugs.

It wasn't long before the rest of the group gathered around us. As expected, they hadn't disturbed any additional deer. Although we had nothing to show for our efforts, we did have an unusual story to tell. And we all had a good laugh at Billy's expense. He just smiled and offered to let one of us cut off his shirt tail, a tradition reserved for hunters who have screwed up in a major way.

Billy's lack of organization and inattention had cost him a nice buck, but he might have paid a higher price. The 16-gauge shells plugged the barrel just enough to prevent its larger cousin from fully chambering. Had Billy's bag of shells contained a 20-gauge slug, it would have been possible to load a 12-gauge round behind the smaller shell. In that case, the gun would have likely blown up when the trigger was pulled.

Later that week, Billy redeemed himself by killing a nice eight-point buck that I had jumped from its bed. It was the last mature buck he would shoot. The location was far removed from his encounter with the buck in this story. Billy stubbornly maintained that the two bucks were one and the same. While that was certainly possible, I had my doubts. In any event, the tale of Billy's mishap with the wrong shotgun shells is likely to endure at least as long as some of his more noteworthy achievements.

++++++++

John Dupuis and I have known each other for almost thirty years. We first became acquainted when I moved to the same area of town in the mid-1980s. Like any relationship, the early days bear almost no resemblance to the mature product.

At first, the only things we had in common were our zip code and our mutual love of the outdoors. While I spent the majority of my hunting season in Windsor in the company of my father and Al Cady, John usually teamed up with Bud Hassett to hunt closer to home. Nevertheless, John and I occasionally hunted the same places, competing for the same deer. Besides the geographical overlap, we both took our hunting very seriously, which fostered a natural—albeit not completely altruistic—desire in each of us to be the more successful hunter. In fact, an independent observer might have deemed us to be more competitors than friends during the early years.

We always respected each other, though, and as time passed our relationship gradually evolved. John's primary hunting partner eventually moved to Florida, while the natural effects of aging forced my traditional cohorts to inexorably reduce the time they spent in the woods. And so, John and I filled these voids by occasionally hunting together.

The two of us discovered that we had perfectly complementary hunting styles. I liked to roam, while John was primarily a patient and persistent stander with few equals. As a result, we began to pair up more often. John and I knew a lot of the same deer country like the backs of our hands. If there was a piece of land which was more familiar to one of us, the other would eagerly invest the time to become more knowledgeable.

Without consciously thinking about it, John and I gradually gravitated towards each other and began to pool our talents on a regular basis. These days, we still hunt independently on occasion, but more often than not we hunt together. At this stage of our lives, whether in the woods or elsewhere, I think it's fair to say that John would do almost anything to help me. Naturally, the reverse is equally true: I would perform almost any task in order to assist John (emphasis on almost).

Two years ago, during the shotgun season, John called me well after dark. At last light on one of his late-afternoon sits, he had a buck approach his stand. He took the shot and the deer disappeared into the dusk, apparently hit well. John asked for my help in retrieving the buck, and I was more than happy to assist. Before proceeding, we took the time to gather up the assorted headlamps and flashlights which would facilitate our search.

Even with the sun having long since set, the evening remained quite warm. As we began our effort, the temperature hovered in the mid-50s and the mercury wasn't expected to drop much overnight. The potential for meat spoilage was a concern due to the warmer-than-normal conditions. Not surprisingly, the ground was bare. If we were to locate the deer, we would have to depend on a decent blood trail, attention to detail and a little luck.

John and I spent nearly two hours looking in vain for the buck. We just couldn't seem to find the blood sign we had expected to encounter. John thought his slug had been well-placed, hitting the deer in the chest, but the lack of blood suggested otherwise. Reluctantly, around 7:30pm we called off the search. We'd regroup and come back first thing in the morning. With the benefit of sunlight, perhaps we'd have an easier time finding the blood trail which would lead us to the buck. Fortunately for us, it wasn't expected to rain overnight.

Weathermen and politicians, you can't trust either group! I heard the raindrops after midnight, as I'm sure John did also. He undoubtedly slept less soundly than did I. The storm's intensity and duration seemed just severe enough to obliterate any blood evidence which had existed the previous night. When John arrived at my house just as the sun was rising, I greeted him by saying, "I guess we're reduced to looking for a dead deer now."

The two of us got to work, and we quickly found some cut hair where the buck had been standing when John fired his shotgun. If blood previously existed at this location, the rains had since washed it all away. As we started our methodical grid-by-grid search of the contiguous forest where the deer had been last seen, I happened to notice a small shed antler from the previous winter. Perhaps that finding would portend an improvement in our luck.

We hadn't gone much more than another 150 yards when I stumbled into the dead buck. If the wind had been blowing in my face, I could have followed the rank scent directly to the deer. The buck was pretty ripe! John's slug had hit a bit too far back, clipping the guts. Nonetheless, I was pleased to have finally located the deer and I yelled my finding to John, who was fifty yards away.

John hurried over, whereupon we discussed what had transpired. The deer had apparently crawled into this thicket shortly after being hit and subsequently died there. There was no way of telling whether or not the buck was still alive while we searched for him the night before. His final resting place was about seventy-five yards beyond where we had ventured the previous evening. John felt bad that he hadn't made a better shot, but I reminded him it happens to everyone, myself included.

With the buck finally claimed, it was time for the fun to commence. John unsheathed his knife while I grabbed the deer's front legs, swung myself into a position upwind of the animal's belly and tried to position my nose as far away from the carcass as humanly possible. In all honesty, I'm not particularly skittish about such things, but this effort promised to be a challenge. At the last minute John looked my way, held out his blade and said, "You want to gut him?"

What I really wanted was to be standing somewhere in the next county. My reply was short, simple and terse. In fact, I only needed two words to decline such a generous offer. The second word was "you," followed by three exclamation points. John, for his part, seemed to take offense at my forceful retort, saying, "I thought you were my friend." I reminded him that I had spent half of the previous night out in the dark looking for his deer, and that I had been the one who had ultimately discovered the buck. I said, "John, I am your friend, but every friendship has its limits; if I were to honor this request, before long you'd be expecting me to remove splinters from your ass!"

We both had a good laugh at the playful banter. John gutted the deer as quickly as possible, and then we practically ran away from the malodorous gut pile, buck in tow. Far removed from the vomit-provoking stench, we stopped briefly to thoroughly rinse the buck's now-vacant body cavity in a nearby stream. We had the deer out of the woods before 10am, concluding an interesting and humorous chapter in our relationship.

As hard as John tried, he was unable to find an independent arbiter who was willing to take his side in the my-friend-wouldn't-gut-my-stinky-deer saga. One person even opined that, had John made the same request of him, not only would he have refused but he would have been tempted to turn his gun John's way—an option I had failed to consider at the time.

++++++++

With the writing of this book well underway, I sought my father's help in recalling some of the details pertaining to our hunts together. I even made a specific inquiry regarding potential material which would be suitable for inclusion in this chapter. Unfortunately, nothing noteworthy came to his mind.

In the course of our conversation, we reminisced about the people we had the privilege of spending time with in the woods (many of whom have passed away), as well as the places we hunted and our shared experiences. With the conversation seemingly at an end, and my eighty-four-year-old father half way out the door, he stopped and said the following: "There's something I've been meaning to tell you."

Both the setting and the manner in which the sentence was spoken gave me pause. To be honest, I wasn't even sure whether the words which would surely follow pertained to our latest discussions or some other subject. I was certainly curious regarding what dad was about to 'fess up' to, so I gently urged him forward by replying, "Okay, what's that?"

He began by drawing my attention to a specific piece of hunting ground, saying, "Remember the time you pushed the area for me?" While I certainly didn't have any trouble zeroing in on the location, the reference was more than a little vague in regards to the hunt's timing. Over the years, I had probably traveled through this very stretch of woods on hundreds of occasions in an attempt to run deer by my father.

He didn't bother to specify a particular year (not that it would have really mattered), but the next detail that slipped from my father's mouth was telling, and it foreshadowed, for me at least, how this story would most likely conclude. Dad rather sheepishly uttered, "And I had a doe permit that year."

Continuing on, he related how five does had slowly approached his position where the woods met the edge of a mowed field. According to my father, I had obviously moved the deer during the course of my travels, because the animals kept looking back in my direction while alternately stamping their hooves. Dad then admitted that, even though the deer had been in plain sight less than thirty yards distant with nary a twig in the way, he had chosen to be a spectator that day instead of a hunter. "I watched them for several minutes before they eventually ran away," he said, adding, "I never even raised my gun."

Once dad mentioned the doe permit I figured the story would end with a bald one slipping away, although I hadn't anticipated this particular outcome, not by a long shot. I wouldn't have been surprised to learn my father had failed to kill one of the animals because he forgot to load his gun, was looking the wrong way, or failed to hear the deer approach. Hell, I would have found it completely plausible if he had told me he was busy taking a leak when the deer showed up. However, I was completely stunned to learn that my father made a conscious decision to let a perfectly good opportunity pass without even firing a shot!

But dad wasn't done. With the cat now fully out of the bag, my father then offered a rationale, not for his hard-to-fathom inaction on that long-ago day, but instead, for subsequently failing to divulge the affair to me. "I didn't tell you at the time because…" I quickly interrupted, finishing his sentence for him, "…you thought I just might shoot you!" "Something like that," my dad admitted.

Although I still was having trouble pinning down the exact date of this fiasco, I couldn't imagine that, at the time, I wasn't aware that I had moved deer in my father's direction, even if the hunt had taken place in the absence of snow. Therefore, I asked, "What did you tell me when I met up with you?" Dad replied, "I said I had seen the deer but they blew by me on a dead run."

With all the cards now on the table, I felt like I was a contestant on a new reality television show called "Sins of the Father" or something similar. Strangely enough, though, I rather quickly found a way to put all these revelations into some sort of understandable context. The summation goes something like this: Get Paul to claw his way through miles and miles of brush, sacrificing his own chances to make a kill, in an attempt to run deer by the old man; on that one occasion out of one hundred when all the pieces come together perfectly and you have a legitimate chance to kill a deer, forget you're holding a shotgun in your hands; and when questioned after the fact, lie about what really happened.

Boy, it's nice to know you can count on your hunting partners! Great things can be accomplished when two people are working in perfect unison towards a common goal. Until this day, I had always believed my father to be honest and trustworthy. Now, for the first time in my life, I found myself hoping I had received the bulk of my genetic material from my mother, as that seemed to be my best chance of avoiding the undesirable secrecy and insanity genes my father apparently carried.

Joking aside, even with all the clues available to me, I still was unable to accurately place the hunt. I certainly recalled hearing the aforementioned "blew by me" phrase, but it seemed to be of ancient origin rather than of more recent vintage. Upon further reflection, my best guess was that this hunt occurred between ten and twenty years ago.

I really didn't think it was possible for someone to "mean to tell you" over a period of decades. That's a long time to keep a secret, especially one so innocuous. I'm sure I would have been upset had I been told the truth in a timely fashion. However, for an offense such as this, I doubt the statute of limitations for my displeasure would have extended beyond a single hunting season.

And so, my father, who thought he had no humorous stories to contribute to the book, inadvertently provided one anyway. Only God knows what other secrets he may still be withholding, waiting for just the right opportunity to bring me up to speed, and how many more years I'll have to wait to learn the details. Then again, given dad's cautious approach to full disclosure, he may choose to take the rest of his screw-ups to the grave.

On second thought, to hell with the niceties and this trying-to-be-understanding crap! Perhaps it would have been better had my father taken this episode of temporary insanity to his final resting place. On third thought, if I hurry I just might have enough time to grab my shotgun and get over to my father's house before he leaves for church.

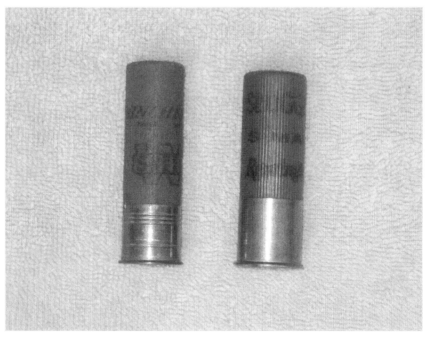

A vintage 16-gauge rifled-slug round with paper casing (l), compared to its more modern and larger 12-gauge cousin sporting plastic casing (r). If you choose to forego the original packaging, at least use a separate brown bag for each gauge.

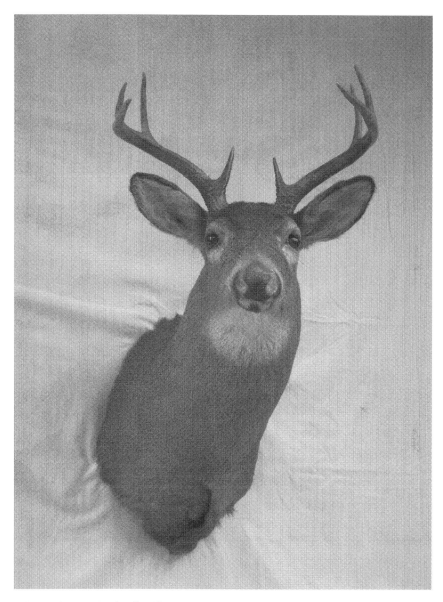

This is the 8-point buck Billy Drew shot after his screw-up with the shotgun shells. I got the deer on his feet and Billy performed flawlessly. He always maintained this buck was the same one that had eluded him earlier.

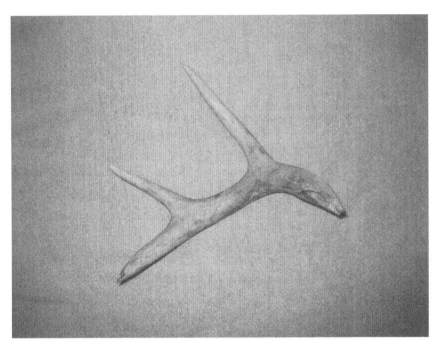

The partial shed antler I found the morning John and I went looking for his malodorous buck.

THE COMEBACK BUCK

This story dates to mid-December of 2010. My hunting season hadn't been very productive. Although there seemed to be plenty of deer around, tracking snow was in short supply, making for a discouraging situation. It's frequently said that things can always get worse, and so they did. A disc in my neck herniated. That unanticipated and unwelcome event left me in a state of constant pain, and with deficits of strength in my upper body. In a word, I was miserable. I endured in the woods for several more days, but I ultimately acquiesced to my pain and surrendered the final few hunting days left in the year. Naturally, we finally had some snow on the ground by then.

I underwent surgery the following April to correct my malady. Two discs were removed and three vertebrae were fused. Although this procedure finally alleviated the pain I had been experiencing, my surgeon felt I needed to avoid sharp blows to the area in order to protect my healing spine. As a consequence, he advised me not to shoot any shoulder-fired weapons for one year. Of course, that meant that I wouldn't be doing any deer hunting during the 2011 season. I actually did get into the woods in an effort to try and chase deer to others, like my father, my son Andrew and John Dupuis. I just didn't carry a gun.

By the time 2012 rolled around, I still had some nagging issues related to my right shoulder. My spine surgeon thought it would be prudent to have those problems checked out. After a new round of tests, appointments and procedures, I eventually underwent another surgery in early September, shortly after returning from a scheduled sheep hunt in the Yukon Territory. Although it was a bit of a surprise to both me and my surgeon, I had a fairly significant tear in my right rotator cuff. Unfortunately, that meant that my rehabilitation would be longer and more extensive than I had previously thought.

Less than three months later, as the 2012 deer hunting season commenced, I was still physically sub-par. Shooting the gun was no longer an issue; I just didn't feel like myself. And after a few days in the woods, I seriously wondered if I'd ever track down another buck. After all, this was the third consecutive hunting season where I had been affected by health issues, and I was a bit out of practice.

My sense of confidence and well-being wasn't helped when I took a nasty fall while hunting with my father during the first week of the shotgun season. I tripped while walking through a tangle of underbrush. Protecting my right arm and shoulder, I went down on my left side with my gun in that hand. The barrel bounced off a bent-over sapling, rising to smash me in the head as I clumsily descended. The result of the mishap was a small laceration and a black eye, which provoked a seemingly endless series of questions from nearly everyone who came in contact with me over the next week or so.

A couple of weeks later, however, things were on the upswing. I didn't know whether to credit the fresh air, exercise or the just the passage of time for my improvement, but I was grateful to finally be getting back to some semblance of normalcy. Still, snow had been scarce and there hadn't yet been any good opportunities to track.

Finally, near the end of the first week of the muzzle-loader season, we were graced with the first significant snowfall of the season, just as my physical condition was beginning to crest.

It had snowed overnight, leaving three or four inches of light, powdery—and very welcome—white stuff on the ground. The morning dawned cold and windy, and the weather forecast promised intermittent snow squalls during the course of the day. John Dupuis and my son Andrew were my hunting companions for the hunt. Before we left my kitchen, I advised them to load up on my homemade trail mix. I had no intention of leaving the woods for lunch, not with the onset of very good tracking conditions, and especially not given the length of time we had been forced to wait for their arrival. I was expecting to put in a "maximum effort" day. With equal parts of expectation and hope, I also declared, "Someone has to kill a deer today."

The three of us chose to check out an area where I had discovered two mature bucks bedding earlier in the season, on a day when there was just a dusting of snow present. The first tracks I found looked quite old, as they were about half filled with blowing snow. Nevertheless, after playing with the prints for a while, I was able to get a good look at the makers. I eventually counted seven does and fawns as they walked through the hardwoods below me, about 100 yards away. Since none of the animals sported antlers, I carefully withdrew and continued my search for any bucks the area might have held. Although I did see another doe with her fawn, I came up empty in my search for antlered game, so we decided to look elsewhere.

The three of us quickly deployed to new country, where I immediately began looking for a buck track I could follow. During the course of my travels, I wandered into two more deer, another doe and fawn. They were bedded downhill from me, no more than eighty yards away. Once I confirmed that neither deer sported antlers, I simply backed away and left them no wiser to my presence.

I've always measured my proficiency in the woods, in large part, by my ability to see deer before they see me, especially bedded deer. This last encounter helped me recognize that I still possessed some of the old magic.

It was now about noon, and intermittent snow squalls of varying intensity and duration were quickly becoming the norm. I was navigating a series of knolls, still looking for a buck to track, when I observed a black object through the blowing snow, about 100 yards away on the top of one of the hills. At first glance, I thought the object in question was most likely a moose. However, after a more thorough examination with my binoculars, the lines and angles didn't support that conclusion. I finally decided I was looking at the root system of a tree that had fallen in the opposite direction.

I advanced another twenty yards where I intercepted a fresh black bear track—a big bear track. Sorry, make that a humongous bear track! This particular print was twice as wide as the indentation made by my boot. Suddenly, I had newfound insight regarding the true identity of the black blob I had just seen and twice mislabeled.

I lifted my eyes and immediately recognized the track's maker sitting on the top of a knoll just eighty yards in front of me. From my station on the crest of an adjoining hill, there was nothing but air and a few floating snowflakes separating us. The bear had to have a live weight in excess of 500 pounds, and he just kept rocking back and forth on his haunches as I watched in amazement for over ten minutes. It was quite a sight!

At long last, the big bruin rolled to his feet and slowly lumbered away to the south. Out of an abundance of caution, I chose a route that headed north. I had covered several hundred yards when I finally cut the type of track I had been looking for all day. Based on its size, I figured the track in question belonged to a yearling buck. I also deemed the spoor to be quite fresh since there was very little new-fallen snow obscuring the prints. The deer seemed to be just wandering around, and given the time of day, I thought I might catch him still on his feet.

I followed slowly, looking for the buck as I trailed. I had been on the track for approximately a half mile when I glimpsed movement ahead of me. There was a sizeable hill to my right, so I carefully slipped behind the contour and climbed to the top. From my higher vantage point I could easily see the deer below me, giving me the opportunity to confirm that the animal was, in fact, a buck. As soon as I witnessed the "branches" above the deer's head move in concert with the rest of the deer's body, I started analyzing my shooting options.

When I hunt with my muzzleloader I intentionally choose iron sights with which to aim. Specifically, I employ a rear peep sight in conjunction with a front bead. I use this combination because it's more in keeping with the primitive theme. My adherence to tradition has cost me some deer over the years, but that's okay. Every deer I do take becomes that much more meaningful and rewarding.

Don't get me wrong; I wouldn't begrudge anyone else the right to select a sighting system that works best for him or her. Some hunters, especially those of us who are older, no longer have eyes capable of effectively focusing at different distances. At some point, I expect that I'll be included in that category, whereupon I'll probably throw a scope or red-dot sight onto the black-powder gun. Until that day, I'll continue to make life a little harder than need be and stay primitive.

The buck stood about eighty yards below me, and he had no idea I was in the neighborhood, at least for the moment. The wind was a wee bit iffy, so I didn't want to jeopardize the opportunity by waiting too long and risking the buck becoming alarmed by an errant breeze carrying my scent. I also had a tree nearby that I could use to help steady my aim.

The decision having been made to take the shot from where I stood, my only other consideration was finding a clear path through the brush so my bullet could reach the buck without fear of being deflected. The buck stepped into a small opening, but he was facing directly away from me. I had a rock-solid rest and a stationary target with an unobstructed path to it. After placing the front aiming bead at the top of the buck's hip and exhaling, I touched off the shot.

Perhaps I could have obtained the same advantageous shooting conditions but a more favorable presentation (e.g., broadside) had I been more patient. Experience has taught me that waiting for the perfect opportunity often results in no opportunity. Sometimes you're damned if you do and damned if you don't. I do know this: I was confident I could hit the deer exactly where I was aiming and, at the very least, that would most certainly break his pelvis, putting him on the ground for keeps. At worst, I would need to reload and finish the buck off.

The bullet did the damage I had expected it to do, instantly dropping the buck in his tracks. I immediately grabbed the fanny pack containing my spare bullets and powder, setting the contents on the ground at my feet, so I could reload my muzzleloader. In doing so, I noticed that there was no snow where I was located, just wet leaves. It was only then that I realized I was standing in the exact same spot the bear had occupied an hour earlier. My single-minded concentration on the buck I was tracking kept me from recognizing the relevant landmarks.

As soon as the gun was ready, I hurried down and finished off the buck. I felt bad that I hadn't ended his life as cleanly as I would have preferred. And while I was happy to have taken the small buck, I didn't relish the situation in which I found myself.

There was a huge black bear in the immediate area and now there was the smell of blood in the air. I took a quick peek at my watch and discovered it was 1pm. Then I got to work, gutting the deer at something approaching "warp" speed, while periodically checking my surroundings for signs of the bear as I progressed.

I decided that the best way out of the woods was to head south. That would leave me with a half-mile, mostly downhill drag and access to a place where I could pick up the deer with a truck. Unfortunately, I would then have to turn around and walk two miles in the opposite direction to find Andrew and John, who had undoubtedly begun to wonder where I had disappeared to. Based upon my distance from them, the lay of the land and the way the wind was whipping, I was pretty sure they hadn't heard my shots.

My concern regarding a possible confrontation with a hungry bear diminished with each step I took while dragging the deer. The bruin was more than welcome to the gut pile, but I wasn't sharing the best part of my buck with him. Once I deposited the deer in a safe spot near the road, I hustled north.

Right off the bat, I blundered into two more deer, which I saw a second time moments later. In fact, I encountered fresh running deer tracks for most of the trip back to the truck, although there were no additional sightings of the animals themselves. Mainly, that was due to the near white-out conditions in effect at the time.

It was 2:30pm by the time the three of us arrived at our trucks, where the driven snow was coming in sideways. In total, it had only taken me an hour and one-half to gut the deer, drag it a half-mile and walk the two miles back to the vehicle. That just might constitute some sort of record. We drove around to where I had temporarily abandoned the buck, threw it into the back, and then recorded the kill at the check-in station. Although scales weren't available, John and I both estimated the young buck would weigh in the neighborhood of 110 pounds.

In my considerable experience, this day stands out as one of my best ever in the woods. I saw a total of fourteen deer and the biggest black bear I'll likely ever encounter. Even if I hadn't killed a deer it would have been a five-star day. The frosting on the cake, though, was my good fortune in taking that young five-pointer. While he's certainly not the biggest or oldest buck I've had the privilege to shoot, he's special nonetheless. This hunt ended a multi-year drought and signaled my recovery from two solid years of significant health problems, making the experience unforgettable by any measure.

Obviously, this isn't a photograph of the black bear I saw during this hunt. Instead, we see a sow and three cubs walking down my driveway, an impressive sight in its own right.

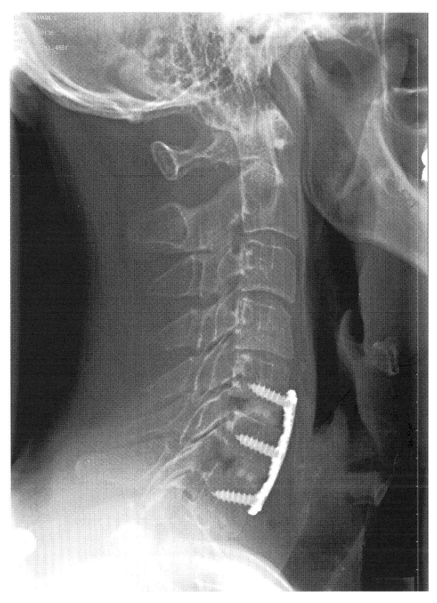

An x-ray of my cervical spine (hardware included) one day after my surgery.

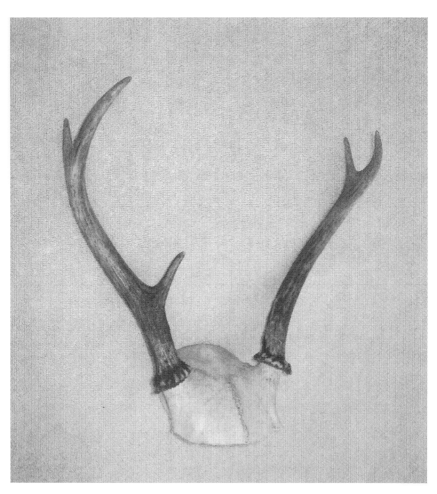

He may not be huge, but this buck heralded an important milestone in my deer hunting experience.

NINE DAYS—ONE TRACK

Winter came early in 2002. In fact, starting on November 24th, the ground was covered with snow and it stayed that way throughout the firearms hunting season, which didn't even commence until December 2nd. Although similar conditions were common around here in the 1960s and the first half of the 1970s, having snow underfoot this early was quite unusual during more recent decades. Most people lamented winter's all-too-soon onset, but a snow-tracker like me reveled in it.

With the snow came ideal scouting conditions, so I drove to Windsor in hope of cataloging the local deer herd, especially the resident bucks in our favorite hunting spots. At one of my stops I made the discovery of a hunting lifetime. As I wandered the lowlands bordering a small waterway, I encountered a series of rubbed trees. These weren't your average rubs, either. Some of these heavily marked specimens were six or seven inches in diameter. In addition, the trees in question consisted of atypical species, such as yellow birch and hard maple. The rubs were impressive, to say the least, but the track of the buck which made them was even more so. I'd never seen a print this big in all my years of hunting. Even at first glance, it was obvious that this deer would field dress in excess of 200 pounds!

The bow season was in progress and had I been a bow hunter, I probably would have set up shop right where I was.

However, the shotgun season wouldn't arrive for more than a week, so I figured this was a deer I needed to keep track of. At the time, I had no way of knowing how long the snow that was presently covering the ground would last.

The prudent thing to do was learn as much about the buck as I could while I enjoyed advantageous conditions. Theoretically, that would make it easier to hunt him come opening day. Little did I know how long the impending journey would be, how consumed I would become by this deer, and how this unexpected and auspicious find would eventually play out.

I decided right away that my goal should be focused primarily on monitoring the buck's whereabouts without disturbing him, if at all possible. The last thing I wanted to do was spook the buck into unfamiliar country or make him unduly wary. From a tactical standpoint, that meant I would try and follow the buck's day-old track rather than his current-day track, for as long as conditions remained generous. Hopefully, I'd compile insights into the deer's life and habits that I could use against him later.

When I first intercepted the track it wasn't terribly fresh, so I felt free to see where it led me. The buck spent most of his time in the lowland where I discovered the rubs and on the side hill bordering this area to the west. I certainly had no trouble distinguishing the behemoth's track from any others, but I also observed one other peculiarity which could be used to positively identify the deer.

For some unknown reason, the buck was dragging a leg on the left side. The appendage, which I suspected to be the back one, wasn't flopping uncontrollably. Instead, the sign seemed to indicate a normal position but an inability to raise the leg fully. Content that I could find the buck the next day, I temporarily abandoned the trail.

I made the drive to Windsor the next day and easily located my target. The buck continued up the hill from where I had left his track, where he eventually crossed a dirt road. In this new area, I saw where he marked up another tree and interacted with some other deer. From the available sign, it looked to me like the rut was still very much in force. The buck spent a considerable amount of time on both sides of this same road before he eventually headed back to the lower elevations. From there, he turned north and crossed a nearby power line right-of-way. I didn't want to approach too closely, so I backed off and drove home.

I began my search the next day at the power line, where I quickly discovered that, in my absence, the buck had crossed back into the block of woods on the southern side of the easement. After wandering around in this parcel for a while, he then reversed course, traversed the power line in the bottom of the cut and headed north.

From there, the buck walked upstream along the bank of a large brook before bedding in a swamp. I found his vacant resting place, and then followed the buck back to the day's dominant geographic feature—the power right-of-way. That's where I ended my third consecutive day of trailing the big deer.

The more I followed the buck, the more intrigued I became with his size. I knew he was huge, but just how huge was the question that preoccupied my thinking. I didn't have much experience with mega-bucks like this, so I deferred to others with more experience. I knew of a study performed by wildlife biologist Wayne Laroche which correlated body weight to track width. Charles J. Alsheimer had written about Laroche's work in *Deer & Deer Hunting* magazine. After taking some measurements of the buck's track one day, I dug out my copy of the magazine in an effort to answer the question which burned within me. As best as I could determine, based upon the material contained in the article, the big buck could be expected to have a pre-rut field-dressed weight of 220 pounds!

Fortunately for me, the snow was hanging in there despite incurring some melting from the above-freezing daytime temperatures. As I began my search for the buck on November 27th, I stumbled into a nice eight-pointer chasing a doe right in the middle of the power line. As I had suspected, there was a whole lot of rutting still taking place.

After a little effort, I was able to re-acquire the big buck's track, which headed north, crossing the power easement once again. For the better part of the last two days this particular feature had been central to the buck's movements, but that was about to change.

On this occasion, the buck continued marching north, fording a substantial waterway before entering a new section of woods. Rather than setting up shop there, however, the deer remained on his northward course until he traversed a dirt road and disappeared into the newest block of country. This piece of ground was relatively small in size and bordered by roads on all sides. As long as the buck remained within these confines, I could effectively keep track of his whereabouts by simply maintaining a surveillance of the area's perimeter. After all, this was Windsor, Massachusetts and not Waterville, Maine.

As luck would have it, after I abandoned the track that day, we received another round of snow that night. And that wasn't at all helpful! I was worried that the buck could have slipped out of his self-imposed box before the storm's onset. In that event, the new-fallen snow would have covered his exit and I would no longer be sure which block of woods was holding the deer. If my worst fears were realized, I knew it was possible that I might never find the buck again. And that was a very scary proposition, especially given how special the deer was and how much of myself I had already invested in him.

After the snow storm, I dutifully checked the bounds of the buck's presumed sanctuary over the next two days. I didn't find his track on either day, which only made me more suspicious that he had escaped my clutches. And if that was true, then I was already more than two days behind the buck and the trail was getting colder with every passing hour. Like it or not, I was going to have to risk spooking the deer in order to determine his present whereabouts.

On Saturday, November 30th, just two days before the shotgun season was to start, and after one last check of its outer borders, I invaded the small parcel of forest which I hoped still sheltered the big buck. As I did, my stomach was literally in knots. At this point, I felt I could deal with the consequences of alarming the big deer; I would have been completely devastated had my efforts to find him been unsuccessful.

I basically decided to walk a line that bisected the plot of woods into two halves. If the buck's track didn't turn up, I'd just have to go to plan B. And right now, I didn't have a contingency plan; I didn't even want to consider one. I wasn't long into my foray when I jumped a deer in some thick cover. My first impression was that the deer appeared rather small. As I examined my immediate surroundings further, I soon discovered what I had come here to see—the buck's oversized and familiar hoof print, fresh in the softening snow! My relief was palpable.

It took me a few minutes to unravel the spoor which I had stepped into, but eventually I was able to conclude that the buck had left shortly before my arrival, hot on the heels of a presumably estrous doe. I suspected that the deer I jumped was her fawn, temporarily abandoned while mom was being courted by her suitor.

I trailed behind the duo as they slowly walked out of the tangle towards more open ground to the west. The sign was exceedingly fresh, and I was beyond astonished when it led me across a large open field around 10am. Only a rut-crazed buck would succumb to such a risky course of action.

Once the field was navigated, the pair jumped the adjoining dirt road and headed into a new section of woods. I dared not follow any further, so I walked back to my truck.

It's quite possible that my feet never touched the ground as I made my way to my vehicle. I guess a profound sense of relief was the emotion I felt most intensely. The anxiety of the previous days was gone, replaced by something short of euphoria. As glad as I was about locating the buck once again, I was taking nothing for granted. I knew there were many possible outcomes that didn't include a photo of me holding the dead buck's rack. Yet, only one more day stood between me and a real chance to kill this deer.

The elation I experienced early in the day quickly turned back to dread when the local weatherman predicted a significant snow storm for that evening. Normally, fresh snow just prior to the hunting season would be considered a blessing; this time it could only be viewed as a curse. I had just spent three nerve-racking days worrying about the buck's location. And just as my fears were receding, it looked like I could be facing a similar scenario all over again. Despite my prayerful attempts to wish the storm away, it came anyway.

On December 1st I drove up the hill to Windsor, probably out of habit and a sense that I had to do something. Four inches of dry, powdery snow had fallen, and the wind was whipping for all its worth. As impossible as the conditions were, however, I just had to look for the buck. The first place I checked was the road the buck had last crossed. I could hardly identify the tracks from the day before, as they were almost completely filled with snow. There were no tracks any fresher than those present, either.

These findings didn't really surprise me; I figured the deer were hunkered down, waiting for less ferocious weather before they began stirring. Given my knowledge that the buck had been with a doe, as well as the timing of the storm,

I felt pretty confident that the object of my fixation would still be holed up in the last piece of land he had entered. I would just have to wait until the following morning, the season opener, to see if he emerged.

Not unexpectedly, I didn't sleep well that night. In fact, sleepless nights were coming with some regularity as I obsessed about the buck: his size, his location, and whether I'd actually get to hunt him for real. Of course, I was excited about being able to finally carry a gun when the sun rose, but opening day posed additional concerns. The woods would undoubtedly be full of other people, all of whom would be more than happy to put a slug into what I now considered to be my special buck. In a perfect world, the big buck would be mine—and mine alone—to hunt. The contest would continue, without interference, until I was successful.

When I rose early on December 2nd, I had no idea how many other whitetail aficionados would be positioned in the general vicinity of where I thought the buck was hanging out. I did know who would be hunting with me: my father, Al Cady, Ken Estes and my son Andrew, who was a senior in high school at the time. His mother, a school teacher herself, had called him in sick that morning so he could go hunting. My father and Andrew were the only other people in the party who were even aware of this buck's existence.

The mantle of group leader had long ago passed from an aging Billy Drew to me. There was no vote taken or formal bestowment, just an unspoken acknowledgement that I happened to be the most knowledgeable regarding the local deer and their habits. At this point in time, I felt like every decision I was confronted with was absolutely crucial to successfully killing this buck. If I made the wrong choice about where to hunt, how to hunt or even when to hunt, then all my previous efforts would be for naught and some stranger might tag the big deer. With leadership comes responsibilities and, while I may have preferred to hunt alone on this occasion, four other people were counting on me to formulate a good game-plan for the day's outing.

Weather-wise, the day promised to be a good one. It was cold to start, but temperatures were expected to moderate as the day wore on. Most important, nearly a foot of light, powdery snow now covered the forest floor, making for ideal tracking conditions.

The first thing I did upon my arrival in Windsor was check to see if the buck had crossed the road since my visit the previous day. I didn't find the deer's track, but I did see other vehicles parked in places I would have preferred not to find them.

Armed with this knowledge, I decided to leave the area alone, at least for the time being, and hunt elsewhere. I knew I was taking a chance by doing so. Someone else might find the buck in my absence. It was also possible that some nearby hunter, having slipped into the woods in total darkness, had already shot the big deer as he wandered by at first light. Only time wold tell.

I chose to position the hunting party in the vicinity of the power line. From my prior scouting trips, I knew that at least one other good buck had been frequenting that area. While my cohorts maintained stationary watches near travel routes, I would try and find bucks and track them. With any luck, someone might get a shot. The morning hunt did yield some positives. Although no bucks were seen, Andrew observed a group of five does.

For my part, I was thorough in my efforts, but my mind was understandably elsewhere. All I could concentrate on was the big buck. Was he still alive? If so, where was he? Would I be able to, at last, hunt him? If so, would that opportunity come later in the day or not until tomorrow?

Lunch breaks were the norm for our group, so once we concluded our morning hunt we headed for Ken's store at the top of Windsor hill. Left to my own devices, I would-n't have wasted valuable time by interrupting a hunt for food, especially when blessed with ideal tracking conditions like these. I carry my food with me. On this occasion, how-ever, the break was welcome. I could check the road for signs of the buck's passing, before putting together a plan for the afternoon.

As I slowly drove along the familiar byway looking for the buck's track, I was pleased to find that the vehicles I had observed earlier were gone. Better still, there were no blood-stained drag marks in the snow on the road's shoul-ders. That would have indicated that someone had killed a deer, raising my anxiety level several notches.

This was all welcome news, but what I saw next caused my heart to skip a beat or two. There was a track tra-versing the road that hadn't been present earlier. I stopped the truck and leapt out to more closely examine the find. As I had hoped, the track belonged to the big buck, and he was headed into the same parcel of ground he had left the past Saturday. This time, though, he didn't have the doe accom-panying him.

It had taken an excruciatingly long time, but I was finally going to have a chance to kill the buck I had pursued all these days. After obliterating the fresh tracks in and bor-dering the road, I quickly returned to the store and rounded up the others with a real sense of urgency. I wanted to clut-ter up the road with our trucks (thus discouraging others from hunting the area) and get on the track before someone else discovered my attempts at subterfuge.

Upon our return, I assigned my father, Al and Ken to strategically sound—and historically proven—stand loca-tions. The track could have been made any time since I had last checked the road, a period of about four hours. However, I judged the buck's track to be quite fresh, made within the past hour. I felt that if I jumped the deer, which I fully expected to do, the buck just might choose to exit the block of woods where he had entered, expecting the route to be as safe as it had been on his recent passage. With this in mind, I had Andrew enter the woods with me. We followed the track until I identified what I believed was an ideal place to post him.

I left Andrew where the track turned to the north. He had thick softwoods at his back and a downhill view into a patch of hardwoods in front of him. If the buck returned along his track, Andrew could see him coming along the transition zone where the thick cover met the hardwoods. If the buck happened to head lower, Andrew would still have an opportunity to shoot at him in the more open beeches.

I quietly whispered my final instructions to my son and started on the track. As I did, I had to consciously remind myself to switch gears. For the previous eight days I had done everything in my power not to view the deer. Now, I needed to see the big buck, and to do so under circumstances in which I could kill him before he sped away. As I proceeded, I forced myself to slow down, carefully searching the brush for any sign of the hidden buck after each step before moving on.

The buck was clearly in no hurry and completely at ease. He slowly meandered northward more or less parallel to the road he had recently navigated, plowing through the snow as he went. I hadn't gone 400 yards when the track took a sharp turn uphill, towards the west. At almost the same moment I saw the buck bolt from his bed, but I couldn't put my gun on him before he was gone. He immediately headed south, in Andrew's direction, and I prayed that he would see the big deer next.

I didn't stand around gawking. I immediately took off on the buck's running track in hope of keeping him more concerned with me than what may be to his front. And I didn't have to wait more than a couple of minutes before I learned the answer to my silent request. That's when the shooting started. Three well-spaced blasts echoed back to me from Andrew's general location.

That it was he who was pulling the trigger, I had no doubt. Better still, the time interval which separated each subsequent shot from its predecessor indicated that there had been a deliberate attempt to aim before firing. That was very reassuring, and it stood in stark contrast to the more common scenario in which the same number of shots might have been taken in rapid succession, a tell-tale sign of panic. Additionally, the sequencing of the muzzle blasts meant that Andrew had been able to see the buck over an extended period of time, another positive sign.

Eager to discover exactly what had transpired, I quickened my pace. When I was close to where I expected to find Andrew, I gave him a "hoot." I don't remember exactly who had started the tradition, but when a member of our group wanted to hone in on another's location, he would utilize this vocalization which was intended to mimic an owl. If the other party was within earshot, the hoot would be returned. In this particular instance, my hoot was left unanswered, which raised my level of concern. It was only in the aftermath of the hunt that I would learn the reason why.

I continued on the track, becoming more anxious about what had happened—or might be happening—at each step. My wait for answers was almost over. As I rounded a patch of thick softwoods, there stood Andrew with the dead buck lying at his feet. The hunt was over! A mixture of joy and relief filled me as I embraced and congratulated Andrew. It was a special moment, one every father-and-son hunting team should be able to enjoy.

My attention then turned to the buck. Other than the brief glimpse of him I had experienced just moments before, this was the first time I actually had an opportunity to take a good look at the deer that had been at the center of my life for all these days. Even though the buck was half buried in the deep snow, he still looked huge by any conventional standard of comparison. I had been almost entirely fixated on the buck's disproportionate size, but that didn't mean I wasn't curious about what he carried on his head. I could see that the buck had decent headgear, but it wasn't until I lifted his head out of the snow that I could fully appreciate the magnificence of his bony crown. The chocolate-colored rack sported ten evenly distributed points and an inside spread exceeding twenty inches. In every way, the antlers were a fitting complement to the big buck's body.

Lastly, I searched for some clue that would explain why the buck had been dragging a leg on his left side. I instantly noticed a large circumferential bulge on the hind leg, just above the deer's hock. Although the leg was reasonably well-positioned, the buck appeared to have suffered a fracture at some point prior to me discovering his track. Of course, there's no way of knowing the actual cause, but I think the most likely scenario was that the buck had been struck by a vehicle as he jumped a roadway. The injured leg looked like it was well on its way to healing. Had the deer lived another two or three weeks, I figured he would have regained use of the limb.

After admiring the big deer for a few minutes, I turned my attention back to Andrew, eager to hear his version of the events which had just unfolded. He actually heard the buck approaching before he was able to see him. The big deer was coming from Andrew's left on a course that would take the buck behind the waiting hunter and then to the site of his previous road crossing, as I had suspected.

Andrew shot the first time at the running, broadside animal from about fifty yards, hitting the deer in the chest. The buck advanced a dozen more yards along his chosen path, whereupon Andrew put a second slug into the deer, knocking him to the ground. Though down, the buck was still alive, so Andrew then walked over and finished the deer off with a final round from his shotgun.

All in all, I thought that level of performance was pretty cool-headed, especially for an eighteen-year-old confronted with such a magnificent whitetail. I dare say; many seasoned hunters wouldn't have held up so well if placed in the same situation.

Finally, Andrew explained that he had, in fact, heard me hoot at him. However, when he tried to respond, he was so overcome with excitement that he could barely pass air over his vocal cords. The resulting sound was more akin to an inaudible whisper than the full-throated reply he had intended.

It wasn't long before the rest of the crew arrived at our location. Our stories were told and retold, but the dead buck received the bulk of everyone's attention, and deservedly so. I had brought along a small camera in anticipation of just such an ending to the day. After a judicious amount of picture-taking and celebration, it was time to go to work.

I led the field-dressing effort. That task accomplished, we dragged the buck to the nearby road and a waiting truck. The distance was only about 200 yards, which constituted a blessing in its own right. I hated to think how difficult the drag might have been had the deer breathed his last in some god-forsaken place more than a mile from the nearest road.

Larry Benoit, the late legendary tracker, was often quoted as saying, "Finding a big buck is the hard part, dragging him out of the woods is the easy part." While I suspect most of Larry's drags were well in excess of 200 yards, his words were certainly appropriate to the circumstances surrounding this hunt.

By the time the buck was safely in the back of my pickup, it was still only about 1:30pm. This was a deer worth showing off, so that's what we did next. Our first stop was the elementary school where my wife worked. I left Andrew in the parking lot with the deer and went to fetch Janet. I lied and told her we hadn't found the big buck I had been after, but the day had produced a small buck for Andrew. Janet bought that line until she approached the truck closely enough that she could see the deer's antlers sticking above the side panel of the truck's bed. Of course, she was elated to hear of our good fortune and enthusiastic in her response.

Next, we made a swing down the road to the Mason residence. Peter and Vivian were good friends of ours. In fact, besides my immediate family, they were the only others in whom I had entrusted knowledge of the buck's existence. Peter and his step-son J.G. were home when we pulled up the driveway. They both poked their heads out the door before the truck came to a full stop, whereupon I heard J.G. exclaim, "Jesus," as he eagerly eyed the dead buck.

Finally, we headed to the checking station. Given the perfect conditions for opening day of the shotgun season, I wasn't at all surprised to see the place packed with successful hunters. There were some very nice deer being checked, but Andrew's buck was the cream of the crop. While we patiently waited our turn, it wasn't long before people began to gravitate to my vehicle so they could view the deer.

At one point, as I was visiting with some hunters I knew, I looked back to see Andrew standing beside the deer, my truck surrounded by other hunters. Stupidly, I didn't think to snap a photo of the scene. When the big buck was finally placed on the scale, his official field-dressed weight was recorded at 201 pounds.

We had more than a few visitors to the house that night, as word of our good fortune got out. Andrew and his buck were even mentioned in an article in the next day's edition of the local newspaper. The buck was the largest taken in the whole county on opening day. I don't know if anyone in the administrative offices of the school district happened to read the article. If so, we never heard about it. Andrew's truancy and the fabrication my wife invented to support his absence went unchallenged.

There are a couple of additional pieces of information regarding the buck that I learned subsequent to skinning and processing him. First, we didn't permit the Fish and Wildlife personnel to age the deer at the checking station because that procedure would have necessarily involved slitting the deer's face, which would have ruined the buck for mounting purposes. Once the cape had been removed, however, I took the deer's lower jaw back to the checking station. The wildlife officials estimated the buck to be $5\frac{1}{2}$ years old. Second, with the skin removed, I carefully examined the site of the buck's injury. What I found was consistent with a fractured bone. In fact, the enlarged area surrounding the break was already significantly calcified.

I have to say, I had been somewhat surprised and disappointed that the buck "only" weighed 201 pounds when we checked him in. To be honest, I was expecting a heftier number based upon track size. In retrospect, however, I came to realize that the actual weight was consistent with my findings. First, the buck was reduced to walking on three legs instead of four. This would cause the tracks to punch into the ground deeper than usually, leaving the impression that I was following a heavier deer. Second, when applied to the width of the buck's track, the Laroche-Alsheimer system calculated a field-dressed weight of 220 pounds. However, that number represented the buck's presumed pre-rut weight. Clearly, all the available evidence indicated the big deer had been rutting, even despite the fractured hind leg. It's not hard to imagine that the physical stress resulting from the rut, not to mention that caused by the injury, would have easily resulted in twenty pounds of lost weight, if not considerably more.

Over the years, I've often wondered just how far bucks travel. In my experience, it's not uncommon for mature bucks to seemingly show up out of nowhere, only to disappear, never to be seen again.

As I've pondered the travels of this particular animal, I'm still uncertain what section of woods constituted his true core area. Based upon the preponderance of rubs I discovered where I first found his track, I could reasonably conclude that was the place the buck called home. The only problem with that belief is the buck was killed eight days later and over two miles (as the crow flies) away! Furthermore, ever since my first day on his track, the buck had been gradually shifting his activities northward. What I'm absolutely certain of is this: If, in the aftermath of my momentous discovery, I hadn't kept daily tabs on the buck, we never would have killed him.

Just for the record, I don't think I would have been any more thrilled had I been the one lucky enough to kill this great deer. By the time the shotgun season rolled around, my greatest fears were that the buck would either go missing or fall to a complete stranger. For his part, Andrew recognized the key role I played in him shooting the deer, generously referring to the buck as, "mine and dad's" buck. That is, until the mounted head was received from the taxidermist nearly a year later. From then on, my name was unceremoniously dropped from the partnership, although I do believe my contribution continues to be appreciated.

Decision-making played a key role in how this hunt turned out, much more so than is normally the case. At several key junctures during this epic journey, I was forced to make choices that were consequential to the outcome of the hunt, to say the least. Certainly these decisions never rose to the level of life and death, but they were undeniably make or break.

Fortunately, at each opportunity I happened to choose the correct course of action. Admittedly, I was blessed. Things could have gone much differently, with the result being that neither I nor my son would end up shooting this once-in-a-lifetime deer.

When one is standing at an important crossroad, it's often said that you should trust your instincts to help you select a course of action. Fine, but distilled down to its basics, what exactly is an instinct? I submit that feelings, guesses and supernatural directives don't constitute instinct. Instead, I believe that what can be relied upon as instinct in any particular present situation is formed from the collective experiences gleaned from similar situations in the past.

So, when I found myself at an important turning point while tracking this buck, I relied on my previous experiences to help me decide what to do next. Stated differently, the little bird whispering in my ear turned out to be me, sifting through the information I had accumulated during all my previous hunts. Even so, there's no guarantee any particular choice will prove to be the proper one. After all, the deer we hunt make choices too, and they experience the world quite differently than do we.

I digress to make these observations because every hunter and every hunting situation is different. There are no one-size-fits-all solutions when pursuing deer. What worked for me may not work for anyone else. Hell, it may not even work for me the next time around. My advice is this: As you hunt, pay attention to detail and build your own data base. Then, trust that those experiences will guide you when an important decision must be made.

Finally, of all my encounters with whitetail deer, this episode is the longest in duration and easily the most intense emotionally. However, it's worth noting that the portion devoted to actual hunting is quite minor in scope. For all the time and effort I had expended in pursuit of this deer prior to the official start to the hunting season, it only took about an hour to kill the buck once I discovered his track while the hunting season was open.

I readily acknowledge that things could have played out differently. I took full advantage of the conditions as they existed and invested a great deal of my time and energy towards the taking of this buck. In the end, I enjoyed some very good luck, a tremendous return on my investment and enough memories to last at least two lifetimes.

Al Cady (l) and my father (r) flank Andrew and his once-in-a-lifetime buck.

Andrew has an "in awe" look on his face as he holds his trophy.

Although this photo may appear slightly cluttered, it shows off the big buck's rack quite well.

Photo by Dexter Mason

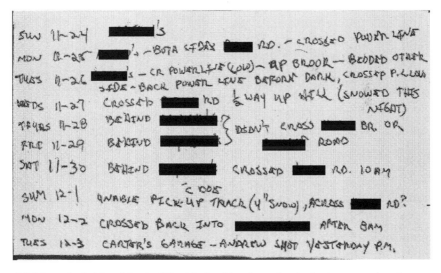

Highly redacted log I kept of the big buck's whereabouts during my nine-day quest.

WHAT NOW?

This story begins where the last one ends. With Andrew's nine-day buck safely hanging in our garage, I found myself in somewhat of an emotional wasteland. The big buck had been the central focus of my life for more than a week. But, while the pursuit had been exciting and the outcome delicious, that episode was now behind me.

The sense of purpose, the anticipation and the anxiety that had become my constant companions were all gone. Sure, I was still basking in the afterglow of our success. That profound sense of satisfaction would endure for a long time. But when I woke the next morning I was, for all intents and purposes, rudderless. So, with nearly the entire hunting season before me, I was forced to confront the obvious question: What now?

Of course, the answer to this unspoken request for direction was equally evident: Just go hunting. But that only begged additional questions—Where? What are the prospects of finding another good buck?

In a normal year, especially with snow on the ground in advance of the hunting season, I would have visited all our tried-and-true hunting spots and taken note of the deer that resided in these places. I would have already developed a pretty good sense as to what animals were available, and where they would most likely be found.

This year was quite different, a complete aberration. My single-minded quest for the big deer left me in the strange position of being clueless. I would just have to do my scouting on the fly, learning as I hunted.

It wasn't as though I was I starting from scratch or hunting completely blind, however. Years of accumulated experiences provided important guidance. And fortunately, there was snow at my disposal, enough to aid my search but not so much that it would seriously impede my ability to get around in the woods.

Against this backdrop, I returned to Windsor on Tuesday, the season's second day. Accompanying me were my father and Al Cady. Try as we might, we saw no action worth noting. On Wednesday, the three of us were joined by Ken Estes for the first half of the day, which started out very cold. After consulting with the others, I chose to hunt an out-of-the-way area which featured a significant course of water that separated two distinct blocks of woods.

At the northern limit, the terrain surrounding the water was rather swampy, consisting primarily of cattails and swale grass; to the south, the swamp gave way to a fair-sized brook. Depending on where you were, the waterway could be crossed using beaver dams or by fording the brook directly. That wasn't universally true, however. In years that featured exceptionally heavy rainfall and/or early icing, breaching this natural obstacle could be very dangerous, if not impossible.

Over the past several years, I had observed a few key places deer tended to use when crossing from one side to the other. I felt our best chance of success was to post my three companions in the eastern block of woods, while I thrashed around in the more narrow section of woods west of the waterway.

I wasn't long into my efforts when I cut a very nice buck track in a heavily used deer run. I wasn't exactly sure how old the track was, but I knew it had been made since midnight. When faced with such a situation, I'd rather err on the side of tracking too rapidly, rather than following too slowly. There's no way of knowing how far in front of you the deer may be. If you approach too cautiously you may never catch up. On the other hand, a hasty pursuit may find you surprised—and unprepared to shoot—if you blunder into the deer earlier than expected. However, at least in this second circumstance, you have the deer on his feet early in the day, and you can usually count on additional opportunities as the hunt progresses.

Compared to the last buck I had followed, this one's track appeared noticeably smaller. But, that was undoubtedly an unfair comparison. My mental measuring stick was, quite understandably, badly skewed. After forcing myself to apply a more objective standard, I surmised that the buck would definitely tip the scales at more than 160 pounds, and perhaps go as high as 170 pounds.

When I intercepted the buck's track I hadn't been in the woods a full hour. Nevertheless, my fingers were frozen from the cold. I was cruising along on the track with my shotgun cradled in the crook of my right arm. I held my hands together in an attempt to generate some much-needed warmth towards my fingers.

It wasn't that I was oblivious to my surroundings or acting carelessly, I just couldn't afford to get any colder, and my posture was a concession to those needs. It was at this particular moment that the buck exploded from behind a decaying tree top a scant ten yards in front of me. I was certainly taken by surprise, but I still managed to fire two slugs at the bounding buck.

Both shots were taken at ranges under sixty yards, as that was about the farthest I could see in the softwoods which engulfed me, anyway. The deer was gone before my ears stopped ringing, and I was left alone to examine the area for some indication that I had hit the buck. After a thorough investigation, I was forced to conclude that neither shot touched the fleeing deer.

There was simply no blood and no hair anywhere along the deer's path, and that really irritated me! My first shot had been taken in haste; I either missed cleanly or the brush swallowed the slug. However, the buck was running directly away from me by the time I pulled the trigger the second time. For the life of me, I couldn't imagine how I failed to connect on the relatively easy follow-up shot.

After figuratively kicking myself for screwing up a golden opportunity, I reloaded the shotgun and took up the track, swearing under my breath as I proceeded. At first, I was hopeful that the wide-racked buck would jump the water and run into another member of our group. Alerted by my not-too-distant shooting, maybe one of them would prove to be a better marksman than me. The buck was initially headed in the direction of the others, but it wasn't long before he swung to the west and crossed the road where I had previously parked, just south of my truck.

For the time being the buck was safe. I left the track and made my way back towards my companions, who were undoubtedly curious about what had transpired. It took me some time to retrace my steps, ford the water and find everybody. I didn't disturb any more deer during my travels and nobody else had seen a thing all morning.

As reluctant as I was to relive my experience, I dutifully described what had happened, recounting my glaring failures in the process. Nobody said anything unkind. However, based solely on the facial expressions I observed, I had the distinct sense that everyone was enjoying my self-inflicted anguish.

By this time, the morning was pretty much shot. Kenny had to work his store for the afternoon. My father and Al felt like they had had enough hunting for one day, so they were headed back to Dalton. That left me. Normally, I would have relished the opportunity to have a big buck all to myself, freed of any concern regarding other members of the group. However, I suddenly wasn't feeling very well. My lower abdomen hurt to the point of almost doubling me over. I wasn't sure what I was going to do.

Before starting down the hill, my father ferried me back to my truck, where I sat down for a moment and consumed a portion of the bottled drink I had brought along. That didn't soothe my tummy, which continued to ache terribly. I seriously considered calling it quits for the day. In the end, though, no matter how miserable I felt, I just couldn't leave the buck with good tracking conditions and the entire afternoon at my disposal. I decided to tough it out for as long as possible.

I re-entered the woods a little before noon. I didn't get far before I was in need of a serious "sit-down." My prolonged squatting session proved to be something well short of a total cure for what was ailing me, but it did help considerably. I was confident I would be able to hunt, at least for a while longer, so I started once again on the track.

The buck was in no hurry to slow down. In fact, the deer had apparently decided to put as much ground as possible between himself and the person who had so unceremoniously disturbed him. After crossing the road, the buck passed through the adjoining block of woods without even the hint of a pause. He then jumped another road and entered a third parcel of land.

This newest piece of country was relatively flat and dominated by thick softwoods, mostly spruce and hemlock. The buck traveled another half mile inside this cover before he finally slowed to a steady walk. The deer was headed west, and the next significant geographical feature was a brook that ran north and south. On the far side of the brook was an old logging road that paralleled the stream.

When I arrived at these landmarks, I immediately spied another hunter standing in the wood road, peering down at the track. At this juncture, dealing with a competitor was the last thing I needed. The buck had just started to show signs of becoming more relaxed, and I had adjusted my pace in anticipation that he might soon bed again.

I walked up to the stranger, whereupon we had a pleasant conversation. I described the day's events and expressed my intent to stay on the track. The other hunter didn't show any particular interest, verbal or otherwise, in taking up the trail, so I wished him good luck and quickly rejoined the chase.

From time to time, I've faced similar situations while tracking deer. In most cases, the hunters I've encountered are very willing to defer to me once an explanation is offered. Whether that's due to a heart-felt sense of good sportsmanship, or because they're ill-prepared for the task and unwilling to exceed their comfort zone, I'm not sure. I do lean towards the latter interpretation, however.

On those rare occasions when I find that someone has picked up the track somewhere ahead of me, I just continue to follow both sets of prints. In my experience, most hunters will only trail a deer for a few hundred yards before giving up, whereupon I once again have the track all to myself. In all human-to-human encounters, politeness and collegiality should prevail; belligerence has no place in the deer woods.

Now free from external interference, I continued on the track. The buck had traveled a long way from where I had first started him, and several hours had elapsed since then. I was expecting the deer to be bedded somewhere up ahead of me, but I hadn't yet seen any of the tell-tale indications that bedding was imminent.

Immediately before lying down bucks will usually exhibit at least one of the following behaviors: an abrupt change in the previous direction of travel, a sudden tendency to meander from side to side as they search for just the right bedding location, or light feeding activity. So far, the buck had continued on a straight-line course with little alteration in speed or direction.

I continued on the track a few hundred yards beyond where I met the other hunter. Though vertical relief was still practically nonexistent, the vegetation had gradually transformed to a mixture of softwoods and hardwoods, and the area had experienced some selective logging in the recent past. It was there that the track suddenly veered to the right about thirty degrees. Unbeknownst to me for the briefest of moments, the buck was bedded under a small hemlock tree less than seventy yards away.

The buck had the advantage of being stationary, facing in my direction. I recognized the deer a split second after the buck noticed me as I wandered into his field of vision. By then, the big deer had his legs under him and he catapulted from his resting place. The deer's reflexes were fast, but not quite fast enough.

I somehow managed to snap my shotgun to my shoulder and fire one round before the buck had completely vacated his bed. Although I was tardy with my swing and hit the buck further back than I would have liked, the slug still broke the deer's spine, immobilizing his hind legs. The buck was able to crawl a few more yards, but I quickly finished him off.

I sat next to the dead buck for a few moments of silent reflection. I wanted to recognize the deer's life and give thanks for my good fortune. The buck's antlers featured eight points and a wide spread, approximating twenty inches inside. I was impressed with the buck's size, as well. Although I hadn't initially thought so from viewing his track, now that I could see the deer, I believed he would weigh at least 170 pounds. With these few minutes of admiration concluded, I turned next to the remaining work ahead of me.

First, I gutted my trophy. Next, I began to consider my options for getting the buck out of the woods. The area I found myself in wasn't completely foreign to me. I had hunted in this general location quite often over the years. However, I was a good two miles from my truck. The immediate task, though, was to drag the buck to someplace accessible. I could leave the deer there and then retrieve my vehicle. I recalled that there was a logging road not too far away towards the west. That trail would lead me to a town road.

In total, the drag I contemplated covered about a half mile. The skid road was closer than I had anticipated, so I only had to maneuver the deer about 100 yards through the brush. From there, things only got easier. Aided by the relatively flat topography, the lack of obstacles on the trail and the friction-reducing blanket of snow, the effort wasn't all that severe, especially for such a large animal. I tucked the buck into an inconspicuous patch of brush not visible from the road and started down the highway at a brisk walk. I was still one road and one block of woods removed from my vehicle.

Before I had gone very far, however, I ran into a local homeowner. I explained my predicament and, being a hunter himself, the man offered to help me. I quickly retrieved my buck, whereupon we loaded it into my savior's truck. A few short minutes later, we transferred the deer into my pickup. This generosity saved me over a mile of walking, not to mention what promised to be a single-handed struggle to get the buck into the bed of my truck. I expressed my gratitude profusely before my benefactor and I parted company.

I drove to the store to show Kenny Estes my prize before heading to Dalton. His brother Clifford had arrived from Maine, so we all visited for a while. Next on the itinerary were brief visits with Al Cady and then my parents, followed by my final stop at the checking station. The deer weighed 176 pounds, which was at the upper end of my estimate. I can usually approximate a deer's weight to within five pounds. The wildlife officials aged the buck at 6^1/$_2$ years, which puts the deer in a tie for the oldest I've ever shot.

It was hard to believe, but in the span of just three days I had been responsible—in whole or in part—for the deaths of two huge bucks! Believe me; that outcome may be a common occurrence in farm country, like Iowa or Illinois, but not around here. Even skilled hunters can go years, if not decades, between top-end bucks like these two.

I'm not without talent in the whitetail woods, but tracking deer is hard work and the margin of error separating success from failure is as fine as fishing line. In order to take deer, no matter how good you are, you need luck too. As I proudly gazed at the nearly 400 pounds of dead deer hanging from the trusses of my garage, I couldn't help but feel lucky.

There is a humorous epilogue to the early successes my son and I experienced during the 2002 deer hunting season. Later in December, just before the commencement of the muzzleloader season, I was in the process of swapping out shotgun supplies for those I would need during the primitive firearms season. In doing so, I made a startling discovery in regards to my hunting licenses.

At that time, in order to hunt in Massachusetts a general hunting license had to be purchased. That license was made of a foldable piece of paper, and it contained detachable tags that were affixed to a deer once it had been killed. To hunt in the muzzleloader season, it was also necessary to purchase a Primitive Firearms stamp, in addition to the general license. It wasn't uncommon for the license vendor to have exhausted the supply of these stamps, despite having the general license available.

I remembered having purchased the general license, but I was concerned that I may have failed to buy the aforementioned stamp. I wanted to make sure I was legal come

Monday morning. As I dug through my assorted permits, I discovered that I had been hunting the past two weeks with my previous year's license. In fact, although I had been totally unaware of it at the time, I had used a tag from this out-of-date piece of paper from 2001 to register the buck that was the subject of this story!

I guess my obsession with Andrew's nine-day buck had distracted me from swapping the prior year's paperwork for the current version in a timely manner. That was my mistake. However, the attendant at the checking station had accepted this bogus documentation without even so much as a raised eyebrow.

At first, I chuckled at my inadvertent error, compounded by the inattention of the state official. On second thought, though, I was concerned that this dual mistake might somehow come back to haunt me. I didn't want anyone to think I was trying to get away with something illegal. Despite my earlier worries, I had in my possession the current year's license, as well as the corresponding muzzleloader stamp. I finally decided that the best course of action was to return to the checking station and explain what had transpired.

This time, I spoke to a different person. As I explained the situation, a look of surprise and embarrassment flashed across the gentleman's face, whereupon he rather sheepishly inquired, "It wasn't me, was it?"

The official was relieved when I was able to confirm that he hadn't been the one to screw up, whereupon we both enjoyed a good laugh. I filled out a tag from my 2002 license and handed it over. A small bookkeeping correction was then made so that the license numbers were consistent throughout the records, and I was on my way. Just like that, two honest mistakes were corrected with the help of a little ink and some WiteOut®.

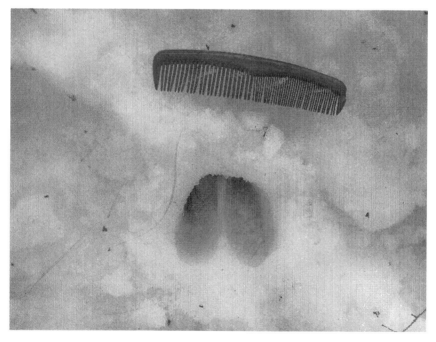

Rounded toes and a blocky, heart-shaped appearance exemplify the track of a mature buck. This one's a little smaller than that belonging to the buck featured in this story. Still, this deer would weigh about 160 pounds.

Commonwealth of Massachusetts
Division of Fisheries & Wildlife

059165   **2007**

Name _PAUL C. CARTER_   YES NO
                                          U.S. Citizen

Address _384 GRANGE HALL_   RD   M F
                                          Sex

Town _DALTON_   State _MA_ Zip _01226_
Valid From   To   _12-31-07_

Eyes	Hair	Height	Weight	Date of Birth	Mo.	Day	Year
BL	BRN	5-10	140				

Telephone _413·684-0634_   Birthplace _PITTSF MA_

Date, Time Issued _10-16-07 2:30_   City,Town Where Issued   TOWN CLERK OF DALTON

License Agent Name   F.I.D. / A.G.P. #

_28.⁵⁰_ _H_ _I_   Original License No.   Class

Fee Paid   License Class

I hereby certify, under penalty of perjury, that the data and statements made on this license are true, and that I paid the above fee, and that I have not been prohibited by any legal decision resulting in a violation of Chapter 131 or any provisions thereof, from holding a license of the class specified hereon during the period this license is valid. **License expires 12/31/2007 unless otherwise noted.**

Minor 1 2 3   *Not Valid Until Signed*   Yes No
                                                 Land Stamp
L Prior License or Cert. #   Year   Sold
    _761876_   _06_ HIP#

My hunting license and Primitive Firearms stamp from 2007. When I shot the buck in this story, I inadvertently tagged the deer with an invalid license from the prior year (2001). The attendant failed to notice my error.

Lead taken from the buck while skinning and processing the meat. I wouldn't want to be struck with a 12-gauge slug.

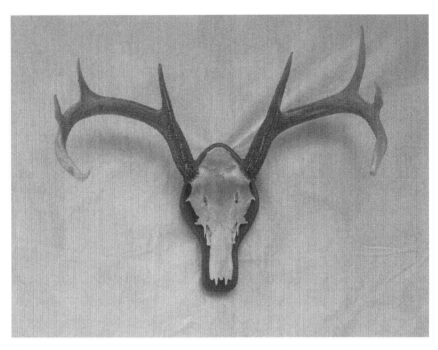

Eight points, 176 pounds and 6 1/2 years old: An ancient monarch by any standard.

AUTHOR'S BIOGRAPHY

Paul C. Carter has been an avid big-game hunter for more than forty years. Like many others, the first animal he hunted was the white-tailed deer. Paul is a dedicated deer-tracking enthusiast and he has written a book on that subject. In addition to his exploits in pursuit of North America's most hunted animal, Paul has hunted and taken numerous big-game animals from Mexico to Alaska, many with a muzzle-loading rifle. Besides whitetails, his other hunting passion is wild sheep, and the mountains they inhabit. He has three Grand Slams® of North American wild sheep to his credit, two of which were accomplished using a muzzleloader sporting open sights—the only occasions when this feat is believed to have been achieved by a hunter.

Paul is married to Janet, his wife of thirty-nine years. They have two grown sons and currently live in Dalton, Massachusetts, where they enjoy their country home and the wildlife that frequents the property—especially the deer.

Visit Paul on the web @ www.paulccarter.com

Other Books—*Tracking Whitetails: Answers to Your Questions;*
Great Shot!: A Guide to Acquiring Shooting Skills For Big-Game Hunters;
Sheep Hunts: One Man's Journeys to the High Country

Made in the USA
Charleston, SC
07 August 2014